ACCEPTANCE AND COMMITMENT THERAPY FOR CHRISTIAN CLIENTS

Acceptance and Commitment Therapy for Christian Clients is an indispensable companion to *Faith-Based ACT for Christian Clients*. The workbook offers a basic overview of the goals of ACT, including concepts that overlap with Christianity. Chapters devoted to each of the six ACT processes include biblical examples, equivalent concepts from the writings of early desert Christians, worksheets for clients to better understand and apply the material, and strategies for clients to integrate a Christian worldview with the ACT-based processes. Each chapter also includes several exercises devoted to contemplative prayer and other psychospiritual interventions.

Joshua J. Knabb, PsyD, ABPP, is chair of the behavioral sciences department, director of the master's program in counseling psychology, and assistant professor of psychology in the division of online and professional studies at California Baptist University.

ACCEPTANCE AND COMMITMENT THERAPY FOR CHRISTIAN CLIENTS

A Faith-Based Workbook

Joshua J. Knabb

Foreword by Mark R. McMinn

Routledge
Taylor & Francis Group

NEW YORK AND LONDON

First published 2017
by Routledge
711 Third Avenue, New York, NY 10017

and by Routledge
2 Park Square, Milton Park, Abingdon, Oxon, OX14 4RN

Routledge is an imprint of the Taylor & Francis Group, an informa business

Library of Congress Cataloging in Publication Data

Names: Knabb, Joshua J., author.
Title: Acceptance and commitment therapy for Christian clients:
a faith-based workbook / Joshua J. Knabb.
Description: New York, NY: Routledge, [2017] | Includes bibliographical
references and index.
Identifiers: LCCN 2016011083 | ISBN 9781138684867 (hbk: alk. paper) |
ISBN 9781138684874 (pbk: alk. paper) | ISBN 9781315537221 (ebk)
Subjects: LCSH: Acceptance and commitment therapy. |
Psychotherapy patients—Religious life. | Psychotherapy patients—
Religious life—Problems, exercises, etc.
Classification: LCC RC489.A32 K528 2017 | DDC 616.89/1425—dc23
LC record available at http://lccn.loc.gov/2016011083

ISBN: 978-1-138-68486-7 (hbk)
ISBN: 978-1-138-68487-4 (pbk)
ISBN: 978-1-315-53722-1 (ebk)

Typeset in Univers
by codeMantra

This book is dedicated to my mother, Susan, who introduced me to Jesus at a very young age, planting seeds of faith in my childhood that did not sprout until I experienced the inevitable pain of daily living in my adult years.

Contents

xiii   Foreword

xv   Acknowledgments

1   **Introduction**

17   **Chapter 1: Psychological Pain in Contemporary Western Society**

17   Introduction

17   The Characteristics of Emotional Disorders

20   Distress and Impairment in Functioning

21   Psychological Pain in the Bible

22   Exercise: Identifying Verses in the Bible that Emphasize Psychological Pain

23   "My Symptoms Are a Stumbling Block"

24   Exercise: Listing Your Current Symptoms Getting in the Way of Living Life

25   Following Jesus as One of the Twelve Disciples

26   Exercise: The 13th Disciple—Imagining a Life Devoted to Following Jesus Wherever He Wants You to Go

27   Conclusion

28   References

29   **Chapter 2: Avoidance as an Ineffective Coping Strategy**

29   Introduction

29   A Definition of Avoidance

31   Major Types of Avoidance

32   Exercise: Identifying Avoidance

33   Avoidance in the Bible

34   Avoidance Sayings Among the Early Desert Christians

35   Avoidance Metaphors

37   Creative Hopelessness with God: Moving from Avoidance to Acceptance

39	Exercise: Identifying Avoidance Strategies that Keep You Stuck
40	Exercise: Placing Your Avoidance Strategies on the Proverbial Altar
41	Exercise: Cultivating Acceptance by Writing Your Own Lament to God
42	Conclusion
44	References

45	**Chapter 3:**	**Cognitive Defusion and Watchfulness with Thinking**
45		Introduction
45		ACT and Cognitive Defusion
50		Early Desert Christians and Watchfulness
51		The Jesus Prayer: An Introduction
52		Watchfulness in the Bible
54		Watchfulness and the Mary Mode
55		Watchfulness and Emotional Disorders
56		Watchfulness Metaphors
57		Exercise: Eating from the Tree of Knowledge of Good and Evil
58		Exercise: Identifying Judgmental, Pharisaic Thoughts
59		Exercise: Leaning on God's Understanding
60		Exercise: The Jesus Prayer
62		Exercise: Surrendering Your Lamp to God
64		Exercise: Watching Your Thoughts with Jesus
65		Conclusion
67		References

69	**Chapter 4:**	**Acceptance and Endurance with Emotions**
69		Introduction
70		ACT's Acceptance Process
72		Early Desert Christians and Endurance
73		Endurance in the Bible
74		Endurance and the Mary Mode
75		Endurance Metaphors
76		Exercise: Listing Distressing Emotions You Have Tried to Avoid

77   Exercise: Enduring Emotions in the "Cell"
79   Exercise: Be Still
80   Exercise: Centering Prayer with a Prayer Word
84   Exercise: The Welcoming Prayer
85   Exercise: Sitting at the Feet of Jesus
86   Conclusion
87   References

89   **Chapter 5: Present-Moment Awareness and Stillness and Silence with God**
89   Introduction
89   ACT's Present-Moment Awareness Process
93   Early Desert Christians and Stillness and Silence with God
96   Stillness and Silence and the Mary Mode
97   Stillness and Silence and Emotional Disorders
97   Stillness and Silence Metaphors
98   Exercise: "Staying Put" in Your Cell
100   Exercise: Floating on the Ark with Inner Stillness and Silence
101   Exercise: The Jesus Prayer
102   Exercise: Centering Prayer with the Breath
103   Exercise: *Lectio Divina*
104   Exercise: Reflections on a Mountain Lake
106   Conclusion
107   References

109 **Chapter 6: The Observing Self and Awareness of the Contemplative Self**
109   Introduction
110   ACT's Observing Self Process
114   Early Desert Christians and the Contemplative Self
115   The Contemplative Self as a "Little Radio"
116   Sayings from the *Philokalia* on the *Nous*
117   The Contemplative Self and the Mary Mode
117   The Contemplative Self and Emotional Disorders
118   The Contemplative Self and the "Being" Mode
119   Exercise: Directly Experiencing God
120   The Contemplative Self Metaphors

Contents

121	Exercise: Getting to Know My Storied Self
122	Exercise: Setting Down the Camera to Look Up at Jesus
124	Exercise: Letting Go of the False Self
126	Exercise: The Jesus Prayer
127	Conclusion
128	References
129	**Chapter 7: Values and Christian Virtues**
129	Introduction
130	ACT's Values Process
132	Early Desert Christians and Virtues
135	Exercise: Detachment as a Central Desert Virtue
137	The Freedom to Choose Virtues
138	Virtues in the Bible
139	Virtues and the Martha Mode
139	The Teachings of Jesus as a Guide for Life
140	Virtues, the Teachings of Jesus, and Emotional Disorders
141	Exercise: The Wise Builder
141	Virtues Metaphors
142	Exercise: Starting the Journey
144	Exercise: Identifying Christian Virtues in the Bible
144	Exercise: My Favorite Character in the Bible
145	Exercise: Jesus' Teachings from the Sermon on the Mount
146	Exercise: Standing Before God
146	Exercise: Christian Virtues in Major Life Areas
147	Exercise: Connecting to the Process of Following Jesus
149	Exercise: Linking Virtues to Goals
150	Conclusion
151	References
153	**Chapter 8: Committed Action and Following Jesus**
153	Introduction
154	ACT's Committed Action Process
155	Willingness, Grace, and the Parable of the Lost Son

157   Committed Action and Grace: A Unique
       Perspectle from the Apostle Paul
158   Early Desert Christians and Virtue-Based Action
159   Jesus and Virtue-Based Action
160   Martha and Virtue-Based Action
161   Virtue-Based Action Metaphors
162   Virtue-Based Action and Emotional Disorders
164   Exercise: The Vine and the Branches
165   Exercise: Writing Your Own Gospel Account
166   Exercise: Are You Willing to Walk on Water?
168   Exercise: Barriers to Action
169   Exercise: *FEAR* and *ACT* for Christians
170   Exercise: Jesus Has Prepared a Place for You
171   Conclusion
173   References

175   Index

Foreword

There are two things I have come to appreciate in recent years. Well, there are far more than two, but I'll only mention two in this brief foreword. The first is Acceptance and Commitment Therapy (ACT). Though I knew ACT existed and even had colleagues tell me that I needed to learn about it because my work in cognitive therapy reminded them of ACT, it wasn't until four years ago that I became a serious learner of ACT. Since then I've attended workshops, read the outcome literature, watched ACT videos, spoken with one of the founders of ACT, taught ACT to students in my cognitive therapy courses, and written about it. It's a game-changer.

At a recent conference of Christian counselors, a colleague and I were invited to teach an intensive short course on the behavioral and cognitive therapies. The course went well, and the audience was attentive and appreciative, but the most fascinating part was the final session when I introduced ACT. I intended to spend 20–30 minutes talking about this new and interesting approach, but instead, we spent the entire two-hour session discussing ACT. The engagement in the room was palpable, as the counselors in attendance asked question after question. Even the skeptical pastor in the audience who had expressed concern about every other approach to cognitive therapy we had covered seemed excited about ACT. He aptly described it as a counseling approach that is deeply resonant with Christian thought.

The second thing I've come to appreciate in recent years is Dr. Joshua Knabb's writing. Routledge offered me the opportunity to read and endorse his book, *Faith-Based ACT for Christian Clients: An Integrative Treatment Approach*. It's a fantastic book for professionals. And now he has written this workbook, *Acceptance and Commitment Therapy for Christian Clients: A Faith-Based Workbook*, which makes the principles of his textbook practical and approachable for those seeking help in their personal lives. You will appreciate Dr. Knabb's clear and direct writing style, as well as his deep knowledge of Christianity, including the wisdom he draws from the early centuries of Christian thought. This workbook is full of practical exercises to help you understand and experience the six core processes of ACT while deepening your faith.

Being a Christian and a psychologist is a bit like walking a tightrope. If one leans too far in one direction, relying too much on the latest psychological theory of the day, faith is sometimes compromised. If one leans the other way, professional excellence is abandoned in order to speak the Christian dialect of the day—a dialect too readily defined by the latest best-selling Christian book. Dr. Knabb is walking the tightrope well. He is a highly qualified psychologist, board certified by the American Board of Professional Psychology, and he represents ACT accurately and clearly. At the same time, he is a devoted Christian, who understands the nuances of spiritual and emotional growth.

I trust this workbook will help you become more fully human as you move toward self-aware, values-based living. At the same time, it will enrich your faith—both your knowledge of Christianity and your lived experience.

Mark R. McMinn
George Fox University
Newberg, Oregon

Acknowledgments

I would like to acknowledge several people who have helped me to complete this writing project. To begin, my wife, Adrienne, has supported me along the way, offering helpful suggestions to improve the content of this workbook. Moreover, a special thanks goes out to Jason Nieuwsma, as well as two anonymous reviewers, who offered thoughtful feedback on the initial proposal for this workbook. Also, thanks to Anna Moore, who supported me in writing this workbook, recognizing the importance of this project. Of course, I would also like to acknowledge the ACT community, including Steven Hayes, who has worked diligently to strengthen and refine this unique blend of acceptance and action. In addition, I am especially appreciative of my clients over the years, displaying bravery and courage as they faced their inner pain, trekking along the roads of life. Finally, "The Lord is my strength and my shield; my heart trusts in him, and he helps me."

Introduction

The Problem of Emotional Disorders

If you are a Christian struggling with an *emotional disorder*, including major depressive disorder, panic disorder, social anxiety disorder, or generalized anxiety disorder, this workbook was written for you. Often, individuals experiencing these kinds of disorders feel overwhelmed by very intense, distressing emotions, such as low mood and anxiety, leading to efforts to avoid difficult inner experiences (Barlow, Ellard, Fairholme, Farchione, Boisseau, Allen, & Ehrenreich-May, 2011). Unfortunately, emotional disorders can be chronic, resulting in exhaustion, fatigue, and frustration (APA, 2013). Based on this reality, you may be in considerable pain, confused about how to proceed, given that a wide range of avoidance strategies may have failed to produce lasting results.

Within the pages of this book, you will explore a variety of common, overlapping psychiatric symptoms that contribute to emotional disorders, including low mood, a loss of interest in hobbies, excessive guilt, worry, anxiety, and panic, learning new strategies to relate differently to difficult inner experiences in order to faithfully follow Jesus, the Messiah (John 20:31) and suffering servant (Isaiah 53). Because many individuals in Western society struggle with *both* depressive and anxiety disorders at the same time (APA, 2013), a plethora of newer treatment approaches (e.g., Barlow et al., 2011) tend to focus on interventions designed to address a common underlying problem—*avoiding* unpleasant thoughts, feelings, and sensations. In other words, rather than the mere presence of symptoms, the avoidance of inner distress may be keeping you stuck, missing out on the new life that Jesus generously and graciously offers to you in this short time on planet Earth.

Faith-Based Acceptance and Commitment Therapy (ACT)

Acceptance and commitment therapy (ACT), an evidence-based psychotherapy within the clinical psychology literature, may be able to help you relate to unpleasant thoughts, feelings, and sensations with more openness, flexibility, and compassion in order to pursue deeply meaningful values, heading in a value-based direction from moment to moment (Hayes, Strosahl, & Wilson, 2012). With ACT, the overarching goal is to live a life filled with meaning and purpose, pursuing what matters most with an open, flexible posture. This proverbial map to guide life, to be sure, involves identifying and committing to a set of well-defined values, rather than relying on inner distress, which comes and goes, to determine the most appropriate course of action in each passing moment of life.

What is more, as a Christian client currently in counseling or psychotherapy, faith is most likely a central part of your daily life; as a result, within this workbook, ACT is blended with the Christian tradition (Knabb, 2016), drawing from the sayings, writings, and experiences of early desert Christians, who sought to radically follow Jesus by rejecting all of the distractions in society that pulled them away from a deeper union with God. Within their "desert psychology" (Laird, 2006), Christian monks developed important strategies for responding to the inner world during moments of adversity, pain, doubt, and temptation. Given the importance they placed on surrendering to God's providence, trusting him to sustain them within the harsh desert terrain, I draw from their writings as a way to integrate the ACT model with the Christian tradition.

Also worth mentioning, although not entirely written for evangelical Christians per se, there is definitely an evangelical influence in this workbook, based in part on the fact that about one-fourth of Christians within the United States identify as such (Pew, 2015). Under the umbrella of Protestantism, evangelicals commonly embrace an orthodox view of the Bible, placing scripture, which is viewed as the Word of God, at the forefront of daily living (Larsen, 2007). For evangelical Christians, Jesus died on the cross for the sins of humankind, with Jesus' atonement reconciling believers in Christ to God (Larsen, 2007). As a result, a foundational component of the Christian life, from an evangelical perspective, involves literally following Jesus as the Son of God, something commanded in scripture (e.g., Matthew 16:24). Because of this, faith-based ACT involves learning to follow Jesus while in psychological pain, rather than avoiding life in an effort to make the pain go away.

An ACT Understanding of the Challenge Ahead

Originally developed in the 1980s, ACT has more recently taken the clinical psychology literature by storm. Currently, there are a wide array of ACT manuals for professionals and workbooks for consumers of mental health services, with topics such as depression, anxiety, interpersonal relationships, and eating disorders. Included among other acceptance-based approaches (e.g., dialectical behavior therapy [DBT], mindfulness-based cognitive therapy [MBCT]), ACT suggests that painful inner experiences are not the problem when it comes to daily living. Rather, the tug-of-war with symptoms leads to disordered functioning. To be sure, avoiding unpleasant thoughts, feelings, and sensations can get in the way of living the life you desire, guided by a set of meaningful, deeply impactful values.

For example, John, a middle-aged, Caucasian male, presents for psychotherapy with recurrent panic attacks. Roughly once a day, John experiences rapid heartbeat, sweaty palms, shaking, and catastrophic thoughts that he is going to die. In fact, to date, John has frequently visited the local emergency room because of these symptoms, only to be referred to a mental health professional, diagnosed with a panic disorder. For John, the actual symptoms last about five minutes at a time; yet, even more distressing, he tends to be preoccupied with having future panic attacks, worrying about when and where they will occur next. Because of this, he commonly avoids life, staying indoors for days on end, struggling to actively engage with the world. If you find yourself identifying with any of John's struggles, you are definitely not alone.

Here, you will see that John has the actual symptoms to deal with, along with the avoidance of the symptoms, which gets in the way of living the life he wants. Among other aspirations, John has always wanted to start a ministry at his church for the homeless, trusting that God has called him to serve the less fortunate in Western society; however, he also believes he simply cannot do so because he will inevitably have another panic attack, embarrassing himself around others. Over time, John's avoidance of life leads to added suffering, beyond the five-minute panic attacks that occur roughly once per day.

From an ACT perspective, John likely needs to work with a psychotherapist to relate to his panic-related symptoms with more openness, flexibility, and gentleness, letting his inner experiences run their natural course, without taking added steps to avoid them. After all, in the long run, avoidance does not seem to work, preventing him from doing what matters most in his efforts to follow Jesus. Instead of being guided by his inner world, which has been notoriously unreliable, John may need to move in the direction of his values, serving others, which is consistent with his Christian faith.

As this example illustrates, there are several components to John's present struggles, which you may be able to relate to with your current symptoms:

1 Automatically believing thoughts are "true" and "accurate," relying on "catastrophic" interpretations about panic-related symptoms.
2 Avoiding unpleasant inner experiences, such as anxiety, worry, and rapid heartbeat.
3 Anticipating future panic attacks, rather than staying rooted in the present moment.
4 Overly relying on the mind's interpretation of what is happening, instead of watching the inner world unfold with a sense of distance and openness.
5 Looking to anxiety-related symptoms to determine a course of action, rather than identifying a set of values to guide life.
6 Avoiding life, including struggling to live out a set of values, overly relying on the mind to determine the direction in life.

Within ACT, you will learn about six processes (Hayes et al., 2012), which can help you relate to inner experiences with more openness, rather than avoidance, in order to live out a set of well-defined values. The six processes (adapted from Hayes et al., 2012) that can help you improve in living an authentic, impactful life are defined below:

1 *Defusion*: Relating to the thinking process with more distance, flexibility, and tentativeness, rather than automatically assuming that thoughts are "true."
2 *Acceptance*: Being able to relate to unpleasant inner experiences with non-judgment and compassion, rather than trying to avoid the inner world at all costs.
3 *Present-moment awareness*: Staying connected to each passing moment, instead of being preoccupied with the past or the future, which commonly exacerbates emotional disorders.

4 *The observing self*: Noticing the inner world with a gentle, calm curiosity, allowing inner experiences to run their natural course, rather than overly relying on what the mind says is happening.

5 *Values*: Identifying a set of values to guide life, instead of being overwhelmed and distracted by wavering thoughts, feelings, and sensations.

6 *Committed action*: Living out values, focusing on action-based behaviors that are authentic and meaningful, rather than merely thinking about them in an abstract manner.

Above all else, ACT utilizes *mindfulness* to help clients, such as yourself, relate to the inner world with more acceptance, non-judgment, compassion, and flexibility in order to live out a set of meaningful values. In other words, within your short time on this planet, you can live life intentionally, rather than merely reacting to psychological pain and being bullied around by the inner world. With mindfulness, you can begin to non-judgmentally focus on one thing at a time in the present moment, relating to thoughts, feelings, and sensations that arise with tentativeness, gently returning to the point of focus when your attention has drifted. Therefore, you can be mindful of watching a sunset, having a conversation, eating food, listening to a sermon, singing Christian worship music, and so on. The key ingredients, of course, are focused attention, an attitude of non-judgment, and being anchored to the here and now.

To summarize, ACT employs the six processes mentioned above to relate to difficult, painful inner experiences with more flexibility, openness, and tentativeness to live out a set of values, which are well defined and matter deep within the heart. Instead of being guided by inner pain, leading to an overreliance on the mind (which can be notoriously inaccurate) and the avoidance of life, you can learn mindfulness-based skills that will guide you down the path of your chosen values. As a result, your life can be vibrant, exciting, and intentional, even while simultaneously experiencing psychological pain, inviting the pain of life along for the ride. Interestingly, within the Christian faith, there are many overlapping points, which are briefly reviewed below before outlining the main aims of this workbook and its intended audience.

A Christian Viewpoint on the Problem

For Christians, the Bible is viewed as the Word of God, with the pages of the Bible revealing God's relationship with humankind. Beginning with Genesis, the Bible seems to reveal a coherent narrative, so to speak—creation, fall, redemption, and restoration (Beale, 2011). Beginning in the first book of the Hebrew Bible (see Genesis 1–3), God created humans in his image. Yet, due to Adam and Eve eating from the forbidden tree, brokenness and hardship entered the world. As a result, the human race now struggles with all kinds of ailments, diseases, and suffering. In fact, from a Christian viewpoint, biological, psychological, social, and spiritual pain can be traced back to Adam and Eve's original missteps, disobeying God by eating the outlawed fruit. Certainly, the 21st century is a painful place, leading to ongoing psychological struggles, including distress and disordered, impaired functioning.

Viewed through a Christian lens, emotional disorders are a part of the fall of humankind (McMinn & Campbell, 2007), capturing the impact that separation from God has had on humanity (see Genesis 3). For Adam and Eve, life was originally devoted to God, depending on him for sustenance and purpose, experiencing no shame in their naked state of existence; yet, upon eating from the "tree of the knowledge of good and evil," attempting to be like God, rather than dependent on his omniscience, they immediately experienced the consequences of this decision (Bonhoeffer, 1959). Hiding in the Garden of Eden, Adam and Eve possibly experienced a variety of painful feelings, including anxiety about what might happen next, sadness and depression about what they had lost, and shame about their vulnerable, exposed state. As they hid, they attempted to avoid the pain of facing their creator, covering up to presumably guard against the physical, psychological, and spiritual shift that was about to take place.

Fast-forward to the 21st century, and Christians continue to struggle with anxiety, depression, and shame, often utilizing avoidance strategies to protect against further psychological injuries. Still, for Christians, the Bible describes Jesus Christ as the suffering servant (see Isaiah 53), capturing the inevitability of his painful existence via the incarnation. Thus, rather than attempting to avoid the pain of life, followers of Jesus (at least on some level) can expect to experience suffering, too. Stated differently, because Jesus instructed his disciples to follow him faithfully (e.g., Matthew 4:19), and the New Testament teaches that Jesus' followers will experience suffering and hardship (e.g., James 1; 1 Peter 4), it may be helpful for you to modify some of your expectations about distressing inner experiences, or at least be open to the possibility.

As a Christian, as you wait for God to restore his creation, Jesus has already redeemed you through his atoning sacrifice on the cross (Beale, 2011). Along the way, though, he has promised that Christians will suffer when following him, which likely includes experiencing psychological pain as you walk closely behind Jesus as the suffering servant. Based on this notion, the Christian tradition offers countless examples of faithful followers of Jesus who were willing to endure psychological pain to draw closer to him.

As a result, rather than solely relying on psychological science to make sense of the human condition, this workbook integrates the sayings of early desert Christians, drawing from their experiences to better understand a range of faith-based strategies to face psychological pain, all the while cultivating a deeper union with God. For the Christians who started moving to the deserts of Egypt and Palestine (among other locations) only a few centuries after the birth, life, death, and resurrection of Christ, authentic living was about letting go of all their distractions. They were able to radically face their inner distress and rely solely on God's providential care. In other words, the desert was a place to turn bravely to God for all their needs, shedding the old life, potentially filled with material possessions, meaninglessness, and shallow comforts.[1]

In the dry, silent, scorching desert, devoted Christians began to circulate teachings about the lifestyle they embraced, which eventually led to the *Sayings of the Desert Fathers*, capturing all of the ways in which early desert monks sought to depend on God for physical, psychological, and spiritual survival. For the purpose of this workbook, I align early desert Christians' teachings with the aforementioned ACT processes, focusing on several themes that are threaded throughout the *Sayings of the Desert Fathers* (adapted from Chryssavgis, 2007; Harmless, 2004; Paintner, 2012):

1 *Watchfulness* (the Greek word, *nepsis*): Within desert spirituality, watchfulness involves a sort of intrinsic vigilance, noticing thoughts with an attentive attitude, paralleling ACT's defusion process.

2 *Endurance* (the Greek word, *hupomone*): For early desert monks, endurance involves patiently facing difficult inner experiences with hope, leaning into whatever arises because God is present. This term seems to align quite well with ACT's acceptance process, given the emphasis on letting go of efforts to futilely rid oneself of inner pain.

3 *Stillness* (the Greek word, *hesychia*): Within the contemplative Christian tradition, stillness involves a calm silence, resting in God's presence from moment to moment. For ACT practitioners, present-moment awareness closely resembles stillness, helping to stay rooted in the here and now. Of course, for Christians, the present moment is where the living God interacts with humankind.

4 *The contemplative self* (the Greek word, *nous*): Dating back to the early desert Christians, the contemplative self captures the intuitive self that experiences God directly, rather than relying solely on abstract reasoning to understand him. With ACT, the observing self significantly overlaps with the *nous*, especially since both tend to advocate for relinquishing an overreliance on the thinking, reasoning mind.

5 *Virtues*: Within the daily lives of desert Christians, virtues such as humility and love guided their moral behavior, leading to the manifestation of Jesus' teachings. Of course, virtues closely mirror ACT's values process, which is a more general term for describing desired, organized, deliberate behavior.

6 *Following Jesus*: Within early desert spirituality, following Jesus' teachings was a central aim, with virtues being lived out based on monks' devotion to God. Within the ACT model, committed action captures the ability to abide by a set of values, being willing to pursue value-based action in spite of inner pain.

To briefly review, watchfulness (with thoughts), endurance (with emotions), silence and stillness with God, the contemplative self, virtues, and a commitment to following Jesus parallel ACT's six processes. Thus, they can possibly help to deepen your awareness of God's active, loving presence and to follow Jesus radically, reminiscent of a variety of passionate Christians throughout the ages. One of the most important contributions of this "desert psychology" (Laird, 2006), though, is monks' willingness to stay present to unpleasant inner experiences, facing them with the help of God, rather than running from them.

Eventually, desert monks' early experiences led to more formal writings and practices on *contemplative prayer*, which has increased in popularity in Christian circles in recent years. Within contemplative practice, over time, you can learn to sit trustfully in silence with God, letting go of the tendency to chase (or avoid) thoughts, feelings, and sensations during designated periods of surrendering to his providential care. Therefore, rather than relying on mindfulness meditation, which has roots in the Buddhist tradition, in this workbook I utilize contemplative prayer to help you with major depressive disorder, panic disorder, social anxiety disorder, or generalized anxiety disorder.

Through the use of daily contemplative practice, you can move in the direction of relating to your thoughts with a watchful attitude and enduring your painful emotions because God is present. What is more, with contemplative prayer, you are learning to stay connected to the present moment, relying on God's active, engaging nourishment for psychological and spiritual survival. When this happens, you may be able to increasingly shed an overreliance on your verbal, reasoning-based sense of self, connecting to God directly through contemplation. Based on this newly acquired skill of relating to the inner world with more openness and flexibility, recognizing that God is in control of your unpleasant inner experiences, you can learn to pivot towards virtue-based action, following Jesus as your rabbi, Messiah, and suffering servant.

To describe this dynamic a bit more succinctly, faith-based ACT is about cultivating a deeper awareness of God's active presence, leading to the ability to surrender the inner world to God, follow Jesus in the midst of psychological pain, and utilize Christian virtues as a guide for life. Watchfulness and endurance can help you to relate to unpleasant inner experiences with more openness and receptivity. Given that God is with you, stillness, silence, and the contemplative self can help you to observe difficult thoughts, feelings, and sensations gently. You are also able to recognize that God is present. Finally, virtue-based action can help you to follow Jesus more radically, despite the recurrent symptoms that emanate from emotional disorders.

The Central Aim and Outline of the Workbook[2,3,4]

Overall, the main purpose of this workbook is to help you—a Christian client struggling with an emotional disorder in counseling or psychotherapy—blend the Christian tradition with ACT in order to learn to follow Jesus in spite of recurrent psychological distress. Throughout the workbook, contemplative prayer will serve as the equivalent to mindfulness-based interventions in the ACT model, given that Christianity has its own collection of meditative practices. Along the way, daily contemplative prayer can help you to turn radically to God, surrendering the inner world to him, reminiscent of the "desert psychology" (Laird, 2006) of early Christians.

To carve out this newfound path, the first chapter focuses on psychological pain in contemporary Western society, exploring the prevalence and symptoms of emotional disorders, as well as distress and impairment in functioning as central features. The second chapter explicates the role that avoidance plays in exacerbating emotional disorders, offering several examples of this dynamic along the way. The final six chapters present the six processes of ACT, aligning them with six related terms from the *Sayings of the Desert Fathers* and other writings in the contemplative Christian literature.

Throughout the workbook, exercises are offered, along with metaphors, sayings of early desert Christians, and biblical examples, for you to experience a new way of relating to the inner world, following Jesus in spite of the psychological pain. Before transitioning to a brief discussion on the indented reader, though, I would like to offer a biblical illustration of this combination of acceptance and action, captured in the story of Mary and Martha in Luke's Gospel (Luke 10:38–4 2).

Mary and Martha: Combining Contemplation and Action[5]
In Luke 10:38–4 2, Jesus came to Mary and Martha's home, with Martha focused on serving Jesus and Mary sitting at Jesus' feet. Unfortunately, Martha seemed to be rather anxious, driven to take care of the tasks at hand. Conversely, Mary was focused on Jesus, apparently listening to him with a receptive, focused, and yielding posture.

In this workbook, I believe this biblical story can help you to make sense of the need to blend acceptance and action, given that there are times that will involve simply sitting at Jesus' feet, surrendering to him. Mary's yielding attitude may be especially important when relating to difficult inner experiences, letting go of the tendency to fix, problem-solve, or eradicate psychological pain. Instead, sitting at Jesus' feet involves allowing the inner world to run its natural course, gently pivoting back to him whenever you have noticed your attention has shifted to depressive or anxiety-related symptoms.

Certainly, Martha's activity and attitude of servanthood are necessary for the Christian life, too. The challenge she faced, though, was with being distracted. Therefore, virtuous action is a vital part of Christian living. After all, Jesus is the perfect example of a humble servant. Above all else, knowing *when* to sit at his feet, versus *when* to serve, is the most important part of daily living.

Over the last 1,500 years or so, many writers in the Christian tradition have pointed to the story of Mary and Martha to contrast the contemplative and active life (see Cutler, 2003). Within a state of contemplation, practitioners are sitting in silence with God. On the other hand, serving Jesus (as well as others) is a vital part of Christianity; therefore, again, knowing when to sit at Jesus' feet, listening and waiting, is key, while also recognizing the importance of behaviorally driven sacrificial acts of loving kindness to others.

In this workbook, I repeatedly turn to the story of Mary and Martha to capture the need to blend acceptance and action. Sometimes you will be resting with God in a contemplative state (especially when relating to the inner world). At other times, though, you will focus on virtue-based action, radically following Jesus along the paths of life.

Interestingly, paralleling Mary's contemplation and Martha's action, some theorists have drawn a contrast between the "being" and "doing" states of mind (Williams, 2008). Originally applied to depression, the "doing" mode involves a sort of problem-solving mode, focusing on the past or future, rather than the present moment. When "doing," the mind is usually trying to achieve a certain goal, recognizing that your current functioning somehow falls short. Stated differently, there is a significant difference concerning where things are and where they need to be. When the mind notices this perceived distance, you may slip into the "doing" mode to fix things. This shift is especially relevant for emotional disorders, given the distress you are likely facing. If the desired state is "happiness," and the present state is "pain," the "doing" mind strives to close this gap. However, this can lead to significant suffering when you cannot seem to close this perceived distance. Although "doing" and fixing are excellent ways to achieve goals in the external world, they do not tend to work with fluctuating thoughts, feelings, and sensations.

Conversely, with the "being" mode, you are rooted in the present moment, accepting the inner world, without striving to fix it in any way. With mindfulness-based practice, you can cultivate an attitude of non-judgment, resulting in the ability to accept difficult inner experiences without trying to change them. As a result, the inner world can run its natural course, without exacerbating your symptoms by applying the often-ineffective "doing" mode to inner states.

Again, a parallel can be drawn between Mary's approach—resting at Jesus' feet—and the "being" mode, given that both are present focused, attending to one thing at a time. Rather than trying to fix, reminiscent of Martha, Mary simply sat at Jesus' feet, cultivating an attitude of receptivity. Therefore, throughout this workbook, you will be working on applying the Mary mode to inner experiences so that you can focus on the Martha mode in the outer world, engaging in virtue-based action in your daily decision to follow Jesus.

To Literally Follow Jesus

Before transitioning to a brief discussion on the intended reader and goals for the workbook, I would like to discuss briefly the notion that Christianity is about literally following Jesus. In the gospels, Jesus stated, "Come, follow me" (Matthew 4:19). In Jesus' time, students were to learn from their "rabbi" by following the rabbi around, walking behind him and absorbing his teachings so as to hopefully transition into the role themselves (Koessler, 2003).

Given that ACT emphasizes value-based *action*, with a set of values intimately linked to your behavior (rather than merely holding on to an abstract notion of principled living), envisioning literally following Jesus as your rabbi can be helpful in better understanding what action looks like in your own life. As a result, throughout the workbook, I ask you to imagine walking behind Jesus, reminiscent of the teacher-student relationship in 1st century Palestine. By placing one foot in front of the other, acting upon Jesus' teachings, you will be dually working towards cultivating a deeper union with God and living out his purposes for your life.

The Intended Reader

The target audience for this workbook is Christian clients with emotional disorders (i.e., depressive and anxiety disorders), such as yourself, who are working with mental health professionals in counseling or psychotherapy. In other words, it is important that you move through this book slowly, with the help of a mental health professional who has training in ACT. Along the way, patience and endurance are critical as you use the workbook to relate differently to difficult inner experiences so as to follow Jesus in a new, vibrant, life-giving way.

Exercise: Goals for the Faith-Based ACT Workbook

Before moving on to the first chapter, in the space that follows, please write down at least three goals for the faith-based ACT workbook in front of you, working with your psychotherapist or counselor to identify what you would like to get out of this experience.

1 _____

_____

_____

2 _____

_____

_____

3 _____

_____

_____

Notes

1 For a detailed, academic account of early desert Christians, see McGinn (1991). Conversely, for a more succinct, straightforward review of the contemplative tradition, including its desert roots, see Foster (1998).

2 The main points in this workbook on ACT are influenced by the writings of Harris (2009), Hayes (2005), Hayes, Strosahl, and Wilson (2012), and Luoma, Hayes, and Walser (2007).

3 The integrative treatment approach in this workbook—which aligns ACT with the Christian tradition—is based on Knabb (2016). Some of the discussions, metaphors, and exercises are adapted from this source.

4 The main points in this workbook on the sayings, writings, and experiences of early desert Christians are influenced by the writings of Burton-Christie (1993), Chryssavgis (2007), Harmless (2004), Laird (2006), Paintner (2012), and Wortley (2012).

5 Worth mentioning, throughout the workbook, I expand on the story of Mary and Martha in order to more fully explore the "being" versus "doing" distinction in daily living (Williams, 2008). Therefore, here, I would like to acknowledge that I will be adding to the original story in subsequent chapters, rather than solely relying on the text in Luke 10:38–42. My interpretations, though, tend to be consistent with the contemplative literature, which has historically viewed Mary's yielding posture as representing a life of contemplation and Martha's service as capturing a life of action.

References

American Psychiatric Association. (2013). *Diagnostic and Statistical Manual of Mental Disorders* (5th ed.). Washington, DC: Author.

Barlow, D., Ellard, K., Fairholme, C., Farchione, T., Boisseau, C., Allen, L., & Ehrenreich-May, J. (2011). *Unified Protocol for Transdiagnostic Treatment of Emotional Disorders: Workbook.* New York: Oxford University Press.

Beale, G. (2011). *A New Testament Biblical Theology: The Unfolding of the Old Testament in the New.* Grand Rapids, MI: Baker Academic.

Bonhoeffer, D. (1959). *Creation and Fall.* New York: Touchstone.

Burton-Christie, D. (1993). *The Word in the Desert: Scripture and the Quest for Holiness in Early Christian Monasticism.* New York: Oxford University Press.

Chryssavgis, J. (2008). *In the Heart of the Desert: The Spirituality of the Desert Fathers and Mothers.* Bloomington, IN: World Wisdom, Inc.

Cutler, D. (2003). *Western Mysticism: Augustine, Gregory and Bernard on Contemplation and the Contemplative Life.* New York: Dover Publications, Inc.

Foster, R. (1998). *Streams of Living Water: Celebrating the Great Traditions of Christian Faith.* New York: HarperCollins Publishers.

Harmless, W. (2004). *Desert Christians: An Introduction to the Literature of Early Monasticism.* New York: Oxford University Press.

Harris, R. (2009). *ACT Made Simple: An Easy-to-Read Primer on Acceptance and Commitment Therapy.* Oakland, CA: New Harbinger Publications, Inc.

Hayes, S. (2005). *Get Out of Your Mind and Into Your Life: The New Acceptance and Commitment Therapy.* Oakland, CA: New Harbinger Publications, Inc.

Hayes, S., Strosahl, K., & Wilson, K. (2012). *Acceptance and Commitment Therapy: The Process and Practice of Mindful Change* (2nd ed.). New York: The Guilford Press.

Knabb, J. (2016). *Faith-Based ACT for Christian Clients: An Integrative Treatment Approach.* New York: Routledge.

Koessler, J. (2003). *True Discipleship: The Art of Following Jesus.* Chicago: Moody Publishers.

Laird, M. (2006). *Into the Silent Land: A Guide to the Christian Practice of Contemplation.* New York: Oxford University Press.

Larsen, T. (2007). Defining and locating evangelicalism. In T. Larsen & D. Treier (Eds.), *The Cambridge Companion to Evangelical Theology* (pp. 1–14). Cambridge: Cambridge University Press.

Luoma, J., Hayes, S., & Walser, R. (2007). *Learning ACT: An Acceptance and Commitment Therapy Skills-Training Manual for Therapists.* Oakland, CA: New Harbinger Publications, Inc.

McGinn, B. (1991). *The Foundations of Mysticism: Origins to the Fifth Century.* New York: The Crossroad Publishing Company.

McMinn, M., & Campbell, C. (2007). *Integrative Psychotherapy: Toward a Comprehensive Christian Approach.* Downers Grove, IL: InterVarsity Press.

Paintner, C. (2012). *Desert Fathers and Mothers: Early Christian Wisdom Sayings.* Woodstock, VT: SkyLight Paths Publishing.

Pew Forum. (2015). *America's Changing Religious Landscape.* Washington, DC: The Pew Forum on Religion & Public Life.

Williams, M. (2008). Mindfulness, depression and modes of mind. *Cognitive Therapy Research, 32,* 721–733.

Wortley, J. (2012). *The Book of Elders: Sayings of the Desert Fathers.* Trappist, KY: Cistercian Publications.

Chapter 1: Psychological Pain in Contemporary Western Society

Introduction

In this chapter, you will explore the common characteristics of emotional disorders. Moreover, you will learn about several additional features of major depressive disorder, panic disorder, social anxiety disorder, and generalized anxiety disorder, namely distress and impaired functioning. The distinction between symptoms and distress/impairment is an important one, given that ACT suggests that your symptoms may never fully go away; yet, ACT can help you begin to respond to your symptoms differently, leading to the ability to live out the values that matter most to you.

Throughout the chapter, you will be asked to think about your symptoms, as well as identify key biblical figures who struggled with psychological pain, choosing to follow God's plan in spite of their inner struggles. To conclude, you will envision what your life might look like if you were living out the teachings of Jesus, following him each step of the way, without your symptoms blocking you from pressing forward.

The Characteristics of Emotional Disorders

Emotional disorders are fairly common in the United States. Recent data suggest that roughly one in three adults will experience an anxiety disorder at some point in their lifetime, whereas about one in five adults will struggle with major depressive disorder (Kessler, Petukhova, Sampson, Zaslavsky, & Wittchen, 2012). As these numbers reveal, a significant portion of the adult population will face the reality of an emotional disorder. When this happens, it can be a very confusing time, with some adults unsure of exactly how to proceed.

Unfortunately, emotional disorders can also be chronic, with many adults suffering from multiple episodes over a period. For example, some findings suggest that one in two individuals will experience an additional episode of depression only a few months after the initial symptoms go away, with four in five struggling with a subsequent depressive episode after three years of remission (Ayd, 2000). With anxiety disorders, research has revealed that roughly a decade after an initial diagnosis, the majority of individuals continue to report anxiety-related symptoms (Bruce, Yonkers, Otto, Eisen, Weisberg, Pagano, Shea, & Keller, 2005).

Depressive and anxiety disorders, moreover, are often experienced simultaneously. For example, a recent study revealed that two-thirds of individuals were struggling with a depressive disorder while also suffering from an anxiety disorder (Lamers, van Oppen, Comijs, Smit, Spinhoven, van Balkom, Nolen, Zitman, Beekman, & Penninx, 2011). Based on this information, it is easy to see why emotional disorders can be so distressing, given that symptoms of both depression and anxiety tend to be experienced in unison, and emotional disorders often continue to persist, despite the widespread availability of mental health services. When reading about these numbers, you might be especially discouraged, feeling tired of jumping through all of the proverbial hoops to get better. Still, my hope is that you hang in there, recognizing that there is a way to live the life you want to live, following Jesus as a passionate, devoted disciple.

Although you will probably already be working with a psychotherapist or counselor to formulate a diagnosis, the below review is intended to help you consider the symptoms you are currently experiencing. Regarding the actual symptoms of major depressive disorder, which falls under the umbrella of a depressive disorder, five of the following symptoms (adapted from the DSM-5 [APA, 2013]) are required, which need to occur over the course of at least two weeks:

- Low mood
- Struggling to enjoy activities or hobbies
- Weight loss or gain
- Trouble sleeping (i.e., too little or too much)
- Problems with energy level or feeling fatigued
- Extreme guilt or thoughts of being worthless
- Trouble focusing or making decisions
- Suicidal thoughts

With panic disorder, an anxiety disorder, at least four symptoms from the following list (adapted from the DSM-5 [APA, 2013]) need to be experienced:

- Rapid heartbeat
- Excessive sweating
- Shaking
- Trouble breathing
- A choking feeling
- Pain within the chest region
- Dizziness
- Abdominal discomfort
- Hot or cold sensations
- Feeling numb
- Feeling as though the environment is not real
- Thoughts about dying due to panic symptoms
- Thoughts about losing complete control

You may experience a combination of these symptoms during a panic attack, which is an episode of extreme fear, often taking place over the course of several minutes (APA, 2013). Unfortunately, in addition to the above symptoms, you may also be preoccupied with having another panic attack, leading to avoidance behaviors (APA, 2013).

Regarding social anxiety disorder, which is classified as an anxiety disorder, the following list describes the symptoms that lead to a formal diagnosis (adapted from the DSM-5 [APA, 2013]):

- Anxiety about interacting with others, leading to the belief that others will be judgmental or critical
- A preoccupation with displaying symptoms of anxiety to others, leading to embarrassment
- Commonly experiencing anxiety in interpersonal interactions
- Avoiding interactions with others to minimize or eliminate anxiety
- Unrealistic anxiety in social encounters
- Chronic social anxiety, taking place over the course of at least a half of a year

Finally, with generalized anxiety disorder, under the umbrella of an anxiety disorder, you may experience extreme anxiety, along with recurrent worry about a range of situations, relationships, or events;

relatedly, you may have a very difficult time reducing or eliminating your extreme worry (APA, 2013). The below list captures some of the symptoms of generalized anxiety disorder, at least three of which are necessary to warrant a diagnosis (adapted from the DSM-5 [APA, 2013]):

- Feeling worked up or restless
- Feeling exhausted or fatigued
- Trouble focusing
- Irritation
- Tension
- Difficulty sleeping

Distress and Impairment in Functioning

In addition to the actual symptoms listed above, you may be experiencing distress or impairment in functioning across a range of life areas, including your personal relationships and work environment (APA, 2013). In fact, to diagnose you with an emotional disorder, such as major depressive disorder, panic disorder, social anxiety disorder, or generalized anxiety disorder, you must be experiencing distress or impairment. Interestingly, acceptance and commitment therapy (ACT) can help you to work towards changing the way you relate to the symptoms that make up emotional disorders, diminishing the distress you are experiencing. In other words, although the symptoms might not fully go away, given that emotional disorders can be chronic in nature, you can utilize the metaphors, exercises, and techniques within ACT to address the impairment you are experiencing.

Furthermore, you may be currently struggling with your social relationships or work obligations, which impairs your daily functioning. With ACT, you will be learning ways to live out your values, pursuing value-based living across a range of life areas. Therefore, although your symptoms might persist, you will be able to address the avoidance that has likely kept you stuck. This, in its own right, can be a very powerful tool for responding to the symptoms associated with the diagnosis you have been given—engaging in activities that give life purpose can be an effective intervention. Above all else, you may continue to experience some of the symptoms of emotional disorders. Yet, you will be practicing strategies to get you moving in life again, engaging in behaviors that allow you to live a fulfilling, meaningful life.

From a Christian perspective, some of the symptoms listed above are definitely outside of God's original design. After all, God created this world, including Adam and Eve, who were designed to enjoy a deeply fulfilling, intimate relationship with him. However, due to the fall of humankind, human beings will inevitably experience the pain of life. On the other hand, deepening your relationship with God, including trusting in his providential care, can help you to follow Jesus more confidently. For Christians, God is all-good, all-knowing, and all-powerful—this combination means that God is trustworthy and that his plan is best for you. Since God is sovereign, he is also in control of your inner life, which you can hand over to him because of his infinite wisdom and goodness.

In subsequent chapters of this workbook, you will learn specific strategies, rooted in the Christian tradition, to carry some of your symptoms with you as you faithfully follow Jesus. These strategies will guide you towards watching your thoughts with a calm vigilance, enduring your emotions with a hopeful patience, resting in God's presence with silence and stillness, relating to God with your contemplative sense of self (i.e., resting in his presence, beyond words), and following Jesus via virtue-based action. These practices, which make up a sort of "desert psychology" (Laird, 2006), were regularly practiced by some of the early desert Christians, who moved to the desert because they longed for a deeper union with God. In the meantime, it may be helpful for you to begin to identify some of the biblical characters who experienced psychological pain, yet continued to trust in God and live out his will. By locating a similar experience in scripture, you will be able to begin the journey towards accepting the inner world in order to follow Jesus in the outer world.

Psychological Pain in the Bible

Before you complete the first exercise in this chapter, I would like to offer a brief example of the inevitability of psychological pain, as revealed in the pages of the Bible, especially when yielding to God's will. In the second book of the Bible, God came to Moses to summon him to give a vital message to the Pharaoh (see Exodus 3). Appearing as a "burning bush," God explained to Moses that God's chosen people were suffering as slaves in Egypt, revealing that Moses' task was to deliver a controversial message to the Pharaoh. Of course, as the biblical text reveals, Moses' first response was to doubt himself as a useful messenger for God. In this instance, Moses likely experienced extreme anxiety and worry, wondering if he would be able to confidently and forcefully deliver God's message of deliverance.

In response, God explained to Moses that God would be with him. Still, Moses apparently continued to worry, questioning whether the Egyptians would listen to God's command. In fact, Moses went on to share his serious self-doubt, suggesting that he would likely struggle with clearly articulating the message, asking God to choose another person.

As the famous story goes, Moses went on to deliver God's powerful, forceful message. Embedded within the above dialogue seems to be Moses' struggle with worry and anxiety. As the story unfolds, Moses fulfilled God's request, delivering God's message in spite of his apparent distress. Certainly, this famous story elucidates that a central part of following the will of God involves trusting in him, in spite of human doubt, self-criticism, worry, and anxiety.

To relate this story to the workbook you are reading, consider the following. Moses had a decision to make; he could continue to argue with God, who was waiting for him to faithfully deliver a key and powerful message. Or, he could carry his worry and anxiety along for the ride, marching forward in spite of his mind's predictions about the outcome. Of course, he chose the latter, rather than the former, despite his doubts, struggles with self-esteem, worries, and anxiety about the consequences of his actions. In each passing moment within contemporary Western society, to be sure, you are faced with a similar decision—follow Jesus the Messiah, rabbi, and suffering servant, or continue to be bullied around by seeds of doubt, worry, and anxiety. What follows is an exercise to help you identify several other biblical figures that experienced psychological pain, reminiscent of Moses.

Exercise: Identifying Verses in the Bible that Emphasize Psychological Pain

For this exercise, please identify several verses in the Bible that capture biblical characters' expression of psychological pain in order to serve as a reminder that emotional distress is often mentioned in scripture as a regular part of the human experience. As an example, you might focus on a biblical story, one of the psalms, Jeremiah's laments, or Paul's letters. In addition, please record your thoughts and feelings about the verses, as well as what you might have learned from the selected passage. I have already provided an example to get you started.

Passage in Scripture	Reactions (Thoughts, Feelings, and Memories)	What I Learned from the Passage
John 11:35: "Jesus wept."	My initial thought is that it is okay to cry, given that Jesus allowed himself to feel sad for Lazarus. I felt sad, too, when I read this verse. It reminded me of the time I cried in my room right after my mother died.	I learned that there might be a purpose for Jesus' sadness, especially since he knew he was going to raise Lazarus from the dead a few minutes later. Maybe I don't need to always try and get rid of my sadness. If it is okay for Jesus to cry, given that he is fully embracing his humanness, maybe I can cry too.

"My Symptoms Are a Stumbling Block"

As a clinical illustration of the dilemma of psychiatric symptoms, Tina, a Christian college student, presented for counseling due to uncontrollable worry. During the intake session, Tina revealed that she worries from one topic to the next, bouncing around from wondering if she will graduate college to questioning whether or not she will ever get married. Plagued by doubt, uncertainty, and anxiety, Tina found herself struggling to get to bed at a decent hour, ruminating about her day and worrying about the future, leading to very little sleep.

As counseling progressed, she disclosed that she had always envisioned going on a missions trip to Africa, feeling called by God to travel across the Atlantic ocean to serve those in need. However, because of her worry and anxiety, which led to a diagnosis of generalized anxiety disorder, she wondered whether or not she could faithfully commit to this future endeavor. Although she was nearing graduation, pursuing a degree in biblical studies, she doubted her ability, suffering from a self-described lack of confidence.

As this case reveals, Tina had two distinct, yet overlapping, experiences with which to deal. First, Tina was struggling with her current anxiety-related symptoms, including rumination, worry, and anxiety. She was *also* interpreting her symptoms as a "stumbling block,"[1] preventing her from fulfilling her God-given purpose—serving those in need, reminiscent of Jesus. In other words, beyond the presence of her anxiety-related symptoms, Tina was experiencing distress, coupled with impairment in functioning, based on her view that her symptoms were in the way.

In subsequent chapters of this workbook, you will learn about ways to relate differently to anxiety-related symptoms to live out a set of Christian virtues. For Tina, this would mean relating to her ruminative and worrying thoughts with a bit more tentativeness, recognizing they may or may not be true. Moreover, quite possibly, she could learn to face her anxiety with a hopeful endurance, surrendering her inner world to God. Finally, by way of daily contemplative practice, Tina could move in the direction of relating to God on a deeper level, beyond words, resting in his presence so as to carry her anxiety-related symptoms with her to Africa. This action on her part, of course, captures virtue-based living, denying the urge to avoid life because of an emotional disorder that might never fully go away. Keeping Tina's predicament in mind, try to list your current symptoms that seem to be getting in the way of living the life you want, following Jesus on the path he has carved out for you.

Exercise: Listing Your Current Symptoms Getting in the Way of Living Life

In the space that follows, please list all of the symptoms (some may have been mentioned in the discussion at the beginning of this chapter) that are getting in the way of living the life you want, reminiscent of Tina's story. Please try to spend as much time as you need, reflecting on your thoughts, feelings, and sensations that tend to serve as a barrier for following Christ. These symptoms may lead to attempts to avoid the inner world (e.g., misusing alcohol to numb the pain) or the outer world (e.g., isolating by avoiding the party because of a low mood). Remember, these are typically symptoms that keep you stalled in life, getting in the way of the life you want to live, consistent with your Christian faith.

1 _____

_____

2 _____

_____

3 _____

_____

4 _____

_____

5 _____

_____

6 _____

_____

7 _____

_____

8 _____

_____

9 _____

_____

10 _____

_____

Following Jesus as One of the Twelve Disciples

Now that you have listed a variety of symptoms that seemingly lead to distress and impairment in functioning, I would like for you to imagine what it might have been like to be one of Jesus' 12 disciples in the 1st century, as revealed in the four gospels. In particular, try to envision Jesus summoning you to drop everything you are doing, letting go of your grip on all of your possessions to literally follow him. If you can, try to feel the anxiety arise, as well as the thoughts of doubt, uncertainty, and worry. Maybe even think of possible ruminations about the past, going over all the recent conversations and interactions you might have had with others, letting go of them as you looked ahead to follow Jesus.

Try to imagine what it might have been like during the first week of travel, walking along unfamiliar, rocky dirt roads, wondering when you would eat your next meal. Of course, since you are only human, you might also begin to experience some sadness, given that you have said goodbye to so many people in your life. What is more, you may experience some guilt since you have suddenly let go of your responsibilities with a family business or in community life.

As you imagine what it might have felt like, psychologically speaking, try also to sink into the reality that you are carrying these experiences with you as you follow Jesus the rabbi and Messiah. In spite of some of these feelings, which seem to flow naturally because of the huge transition you have recently made, you are now living the life you have always been called to live, walking behind Jesus, learning from him in anticipation of the task ahead—sharing the gospel message with the world. Whether you are walking with him along the shores of the Sea of Galilee, fishing with him on a boat, assisting him as he feeds thousands of people, or celebrating with him at a wedding, the most important part is that you are walking with *him*. Although you may feel like waving goodbye—letting him know that right now is not the time because of the pesky thoughts, feelings, and sensations that are getting in the way of spontaneous action—your connection with him is key. As you think further about this experience, the following exercise will help you to write down some of the reactions you are having.

Exercise: The 13th Disciple—Imagining a Life Devoted to Following Jesus Where He Wants You to Go[2]

In the space that follows, I would like for you to imagine that you are following Jesus in the 21st century, fully devoting your life to walking behind him in the very city in which you live. On the left side of the box, try to identify and list out all of the thoughts, feelings, and sensations that seem to be currently getting in the way of following Jesus. In other words, these will be apparent barriers to behaviorally walking with Jesus, going where he wants you to go.

Conversely, on the right side, please list some of the things you would be doing, consistent with Jesus' teachings, if you were radically following him from moment to moment. Remember, you are one of his disciples—the 13th disciple—walking with him in contemporary society. Overall, just jot down a few keywords, rather than writing in sentence form. Once again, I have provided examples for you in each of the columns to get you started.

Apparent "Stumbling Blocks" to Following Jesus			A Life Devoted to Following Jesus	
Thoughts that Seem to Get in the Way	Feelings that Seem to Get in the Way	Sensations that Seem to Get in the Way	Jesus' Teachings I Would Be Living Out if My Symptoms Were Not Viewed as "Stumbling Blocks"	How I Would Be Living Out Jesus' Teachings if My Symptoms Were Not Viewed as "Stumbling Blocks"
I tend to worry about what others will think of me, which prevents me from following Jesus.	I feel anxiety in my chest, which gets in the way of following Jesus.	I get headaches when I am anxious, leading to a delay in following Jesus.	If I did not consider my symptoms to be "stumbling blocks," I would be a servant like Jesus, consistent with Mark 9:35.	If I did not consider my symptoms to be "stumbling blocks," I would be serving in the youth ministry at my church, working with kids with abuse histories.

Conclusion

In this chapter, you explored a variety of symptoms that lead to emotional disorders, as well as the difference between symptoms and distress/impairment in functioning. In addition, you were able to complete an exercise in order to normalize distressing inner experiences, given that a range of biblical figures also struggled with psychological pain. You also identified your current symptoms, how they might be getting in the way of following Jesus, and what your life might look like if you were following Jesus wherever he wants you to go. In the next chapter, you will be looking further into the problem of avoidance, including the ways that avoidance can keep you stuck in your efforts to live out your Christian faith authentically.

Notes

1 Here, Tina used the biblical term, "stumbling block," defining it as something that gets in the way of her relationship with God, rather than something that leads her directly into sinful behavior. It is important to emphasize that the problem is her *interpretation* that her symptoms are a "stumbling block," rather than her thoughts, feelings, and sensations *actually* getting in the way of following Jesus.

2 Adapted from Harris (2009).

References

American Psychiatric Association. (2013). *Diagnostic and Statistical Manual of Mental Disorders* (5th ed.). Washington, DC: Author.

Ayd, F. (2000). *Lexicon of Psychiatry, Neurology and the Neurosciences* (2nd ed.). New York: Lippincott Williams & Wilkins.

Bruce, S., Yonkers, K., Otto, M., Eisen, J., Weisberg, R., Pagano, M., Shea, M., & Keller, M. (2005). Influence of psychiatric comorbidity on recovery and recurrence in generalized anxiety disorder, social phobia, and panic disorder: A 12-year prospective study. *American Journal of Psychiatry, 162*, 1179–1187.

Harris, R. (2009). *ACT Made Simple: An Easy-to-Read Primer on Acceptance and Commitment Therapy*. Oakland, CA: New Harbinger Publications, Inc.

Kessler, R., Petukhova, M., Sampson, N., Zaslavsky, A., & Wittchen, H. (2012). Twelve-month and lifetime prevalence and lifetime morbid risk of anxiety and mood disorders in the United States. *International Journal of Methods in Psychiatric Research, 21*, 169–184.

Laird, M. (2006). *Into the Silent Land: A Guide to the Christian Practice of Contemplation*. New York: Oxford University Press.

Lamers, F., van Oppen, P., Comijs, H., Smit, J., Spinhoven, P., van Balkom, A., Nolen, W., Zitman, F., Beekman, A., & Penninx, B. (2011). Comorbidity patterns of anxiety and depressive disorders in a large cohort study: The Netherlands study of depression and anxiety (NESDA). *Journal of Clinical Psychiatry, 72*, 341–348.

Chapter 2: Avoidance as an Ineffective Coping Strategy

Introduction

In this chapter, you will explore the main types of avoidance that might be keeping you stuck in your efforts to follow Jesus. In fact, recent research has revealed that avoidance—more formally referred to as *experiential avoidance*—is linked to a wide variety of emotional disorders. You will also read about several biblical examples of avoidance, as well as metaphors for avoidance that can help you to make better sense of your dilemma.

In contrast to avoidance, you will learn about acceptance, which is reviewed in more detail in a subsequent chapter and can help you to focus on virtue-based action. Rather than battling with your inner world, acceptance (which is in no way synonymous with "agreement") can help you relate to your inner pain with more gentleness and openness so as to pivot towards following Christ. To conclude the chapter, you will participate in several exercises, attempting to move from avoidance to acceptance by surrendering your inner world to God.

A Definition of Avoidance

Experiential avoidance (referred to in this chapter, for the sake of brevity, as simply "avoidance") is defined as the struggle to accept unpleasant inner experiences, including distressing thoughts, feelings, and sensations (Gamez, Chmielewski, Kotov, Ruggero, & Watson, 2011). In other words, with this type of avoidance, there is a pattern of turning away from inner pain, given that it seemingly causes a tremendous amount of suffering. Because of the intensity of your emotions, you may attempt to avoid painful emotional experiences through a wide variety of ineffective strategies. Unfortunately, these coping mechanisms seldom work in the long run, offering only short-term relief at the expense of living life to its fullest.

For example, with major depressive disorder, you may isolate yourself from others, based on the belief that your low mood will worsen if you fully engage with the world. What is more, you might be struggling with excessive guilt or a sense of worthlessness, having a hard time carrying out daily tasks. When these emotions arise, your mind might convince you that it is better to avoid life, based on the assumption that you cannot live out your values while you are in a tremendous amount of pain.

Among anxiety disorders, too, avoidance is a common strategy. With panic disorder, you likely experience ongoing symptoms of a panic attack, wondering when they will emerge throughout your day. Because panic-related symptoms can come on so suddenly, and feel quite intense, you may believe that it is better to stay indoors, rather than risk experiencing another attack in public. With panic disorder, you might have a tendency to try to avoid any anxiety-related symptoms, possibly through numbing them with food, drugs, alcohol, or Internet use. Avoidance can also occur with the outer world, staying away from social interactions due to anticipated embarrassment.

If you struggle with social anxiety, you might believe that staying away from interpersonal interactions is the key to feeling better, hiding in your house or apartment in anticipation of embarrassment, judgment, or scrutiny from others. When you absolutely must interact with others, you might attempt to avoid anxiety-related symptoms through a wide variety of strategies, such as excessive alcohol use at a social gathering, convinced that this is the only way to push past your social anxiety. Of course, alcohol is not available for most of your interpersonal interactions, leaving you feeling stuck in your efforts to numb the pain.

Finally, with generalized anxiety, you may attempt to create a sense of certainty about an unknown future by "filling in the blanks." In other words, the cognitive task of worrying may be an effort to avoid the emotional experience of anxiety, given that your mind is actively searching for an answer to anticipated catastrophes. Over time, though, worrying takes up all of your energy, distracting you from your goals in life.

To summarize, emotional disorders often involve both inner and outer avoidance, with many individuals struggling to accept their inner pain, avoiding life in an effort to reduce depressive and anxiety-related symptoms. Over time, avoidance fails to deliver on its promise of the permanent elimination of pain, with difficult thoughts, feelings, and sensations continuing to rear their proverbial head. Before turning to a few examples of avoidance in the Bible, I would like to unpack experiential avoidance a bit further, outlining several types of avoidance, with which you might be able to identify.

Major Types of Avoidance

In the boxes that follow, I outline the major types of avoidance (adapted from Gamez et al., 2011), offering a definition, example in psychotherapy, and example in the Christian life. Here, it is important to note that recent research has revealed that experiential avoidance is linked to both depressive and anxiety-related symptoms among clinical and college samples (Gamez et al., 2011), including Christian university students (Knabb & Grigorian-Routon, 2014).

Experiential Avoidance (EA) Domain	Definition	Example in Psychotherapy	Example in the Christian Faith
Behavioral Avoidance	Avoiding situations that may lead to unpleasant thoughts, feelings, or sensations.	A client with social phobia frequently avoids social gatherings because interacting with people leads to increased anxiety.	A Christian with recurrent anxiety avoids signing up to lead in a church ministry because of her fear of rejection and the thought she is not "godly enough."
Distress Aversion	Negatively judging unpleasant thoughts, feelings, or sensations.	A client with major depressive disorder evaluates his low mood as "bad," believing that his life cannot go on without fully eliminating his depressive episodes.	A Christian judges his recurrent depression as punishment from God, thinking that spiritual maturity involves never feeling down; as a result, he pleads with God every day to take away his pain.
Procrastination	Attempting to postpone unpleasant thoughts, feelings, or sensations.	A client with panic disorder waits weeks at a time to go to the grocery store, anticipating another panic attack.	A Christian wants to help in a church ministry devoted to feeding and clothing the underserved; yet, she delays volunteering at a local soup kitchen because she fears she will have a panic attack and embarrass herself in public, telling herself she will volunteer next year.
Distraction/ Suppression	Trying to divert attention from, or push away, unpleasant thoughts, feelings, or sensations.	A client with generalized anxiety disorder frequently attempts to eradicate worrying thoughts by yelling "stop" whenever they arise.	A Christian with recurrent worry tries to distract herself by repeatedly listening to sermons on the radio and compulsively memorizing scripture in order to suppress distressing inner experiences.

(Continued)

Experiential Avoidance (EA) Domain	Definition	Example in Psychotherapy	Example in the Christian Faith
Repression/ Denial	Attempting to disconnect from, or block, unpleasant thoughts, feelings, or sensations.	A client has a difficult time identifying emotions associated with childhood sexual abuse, indicating that he feels "numb," pushing his emotions away in order to "not feel anything."	A Christian with a history of physical abuse and neglect struggles to identify and share his inner pain when praying to God, walling off sadness and anger, rather than reaching out to God for comfort and support.

Exercise: Identifying Avoidance

After reviewing the above boxes, please take a few moments to think about which types of avoidance, if any, you might be currently using in your life, considering their application to a range of life domains (e.g., family life, work life, church life, other life area). When you are ready, please place a check mark in the boxes that might apply.

Experiential Avoidance (EA) Domain	Family Life	Work Life	Church Life	Social Life	Community Life	Other Life Area
Behavioral Avoidance						
Distress Aversion						
Procrastination						
Distraction/ Suppression						
Repression/ Denial						

Once you have finished, please reflect on how many check marks are located in the boxes above. Is the number of check marks surprising to you? Why or why not? Are there certain themes that have emerged? Do you tend to avoid certain areas of life in specific ways? Or, do you use a wide variety of avoidance strategies, which tend to be fairly consistent in most areas of life?

Avoidance in the Bible

In the Bible, there are a range of examples of biblical characters that struggled in their relationship with God, exhibiting ambivalence, doubt, and psychological pain when facing a key decision—follow God's will or turn the other way, attempting to avoid the inner distress and uncertainty that can naturally flow from responding to God's call. In Genesis, Adam and Eve immediately hid once they ate the fruit from the forbidden tree, recognizing that they were exposed and vulnerable. In Exodus, Moses expressed doubt to God when asked to deliver God's message of deliverance to the Pharaoh, likely experiencing anxiety based on his belief that he would fail. Once Moses began to lead God's people through the desert, there were serious doubts, fears, and complaints from the people along the way, with some wanting to go back to Egypt, their familiar home. In the book of Jonah, Jonah ran from God, struggling to deliver God's message, possibly because of a range of feelings in response to God's wish. In the gospels, Peter struggled to acknowledge Jesus around the time of Jesus' arrest, denying Jesus three times, likely due to anxiety about what might happen if he stated he was a dedicated follower of Jesus.

In each of these instances, the biblical characters seemed to struggle with two salient challenges: (a) experiencing inner distress, such as fear, anxiety, doubt, anger, sadness, or loss, associated with a decision about whether or not to follow God's plan, and (b) actually deciding whether they would yield to God's will or walk the other way, avoiding God's plan for their life. Of course, these characters' experiences capture the reality that life is painful, and yielding to God's plan does not always involve an automatic, "yes, Lord." Still, the examples noted above, among others, seem to demonstrate that avoidance, especially in the context of aligning life with God's will, does not tend to work in the long run.

Adam and Eve were banished from the Garden of Eden. Moses eventually delivered God's message, guiding God's people through the desert for several decades. Jonah came around after being swallowed by a large fish. Peter went on to share the gospel message in the 1ˢᵗ century after Jesus died, rose from the dead, and ascended to heaven.

Although life is painful, with anger, fear, anxiety, worry, doubt, and confusion frequently emanating from daily living, surrendering to God's will is vital for Christians, given that God's plan is perfect because he is sovereign and infinitely wise and good. Among the early desert Christians, struggling with avoidance was a central theme, since they had to deal with the harsh realities of a barren desert landscape, which required total dependence on God. In other words, understandably, there was probably an almost daily battle with a desire to retreat.

Avoidance Sayings Among the Early Desert Christians

For the early desert Christians, an important part of their experience involved staying in one place, which was their cell.[1] The cell was a place for praying, reading scripture, and completing various tasks, acting as a room for daily living. This distinct living space, which is further explored in a subsequent chapter of this workbook, also represents the inner life, with early desert monks developing the ability to endure within the confines of the cell because God was present, actively ministering to their needs.

Within the *Sayings of the Desert Fathers*,[2] there are a variety of teachings on the contrast between avoidance and acceptance, with many quotes capturing the importance of patiently enduring, rather than running from psychological pain. An apparently common experience, monks would approach their elders, sharing with them that they had a very difficult time staying in their cell, wishing to exit. As noted below, these sayings pinpoint the importance of acceptance, rather than avoidance, in daily desert life:

- "A brother asked an elder, 'What am I to do, for my thought does not let me remain one hour in my cell?' The elder said to him, 'Go back and stay in your cell, my son; work with your hands, pray to God without ceasing, and cast your thought on the Lord so that nobody tempts you to come out of there.'"

As another example, a monk went to an elder, who told him the following:

- "My son, if you want to receive benefit, remain in your cell, paying attention to yourself and your handwork. It is not advantageous for you to come out, for there is nothing so beneficial as staying put."

Again, within desert life, there was an understandable tendency to want to leave the cell, given some of its demands. For example, sitting in the cell with their thoughts and feelings, monks likely struggled to pass the time. They also had to face their thoughts, feelings, and sensations, lacking many of the distractions available in contemporary society; yet, as a symbol of the inner world, elders would frequently teach that staying in the cell, rather than quickly running from the cell, was optimal for spiritual and psychological growth.

To draw a parallel with 21st-century Western culture, there seems to be a broader tendency to want to run quickly from the pain of the inner world, anesthetizing inner experiences through distraction, drugs and alcohol, compulsive behaviors, or full-fledged denial about the realities of psychological struggles. When this happens, from both an ACT and desert perspective, "staying put" is the answer, which offers an opportunity to learn about the impermanence of inner experiences, as well as recognize that God is present in the "cell," resulting in an increased willingness to surrender to him.

Avoidance Metaphors

Within ACT, metaphors are often used as a way to paint a vibrant picture, beyond mere lists or abstract descriptions of concepts, offering a more experiential strategy for learning new material (Hayes, Strosahl, & Wilson, 1999). One way to metaphorically make sense of the problem of avoidance involves ACT's "clean" versus "dirty" pain metaphor (Hayes, Strosahl, & Wilson, 2012). To begin, "clean" pain captures the original experience of inner distress; for emotional disorders, this encompasses the unpleasant thoughts, feelings, and sensations associated with depression or anxiety. On the other hand, "dirty" pain is defined as the pain associated with trying to avoid the "clean" pain. "Dirty" pain, moreover, can involve strategies designed to try to control or manage, as well as fully eradicate, the pain.

Overall, you may be struggling with the symptoms of emotional disorders, such as low mood or worry. To make matters worse, you might also be suffering from the pain of avoiding life, missing out on the plan God has for you. Thus, rather than only dealing with the low mood, for example, you are feeling the pain of social isolation, watching *other people* pursue and deepen meaningful relationships.

As a biblical parallel, "clean" pain is consistent with Jesus' psychological pain in the gospels (after all, although he is the Son of God, he lived a fully human life via the incarnation), whereas "dirty" pain seems to resemble Peter's pain when he denied Jesus three times.[3] For Jesus, life was about pursuing God's will from moment to moment, culminating with the experience of tremendous psychological and physical pain on the cross. Prior to the crucifixion, he experienced overwhelming anguish, asking God to "take [the] cup" from him; yet, he prayed to the Father that God's will would be carried out, submitting to God's plan for his short life on Earth (see Luke 22). Conversely, Peter struggled to acknowledge Jesus three times, weeping "bitterly" after he realized Jesus had accurately predicted his three denials (see Luke 22).

In the gospels, Jesus' short life was about virtue-based action, following the will of his Father in each passing moment. Although he most certainly experienced "clean" pain—at times weeping, experiencing anguish, and expressing anger in the four gospel accounts—he went on to live out his God-given purpose. On the other hand, Peter seemingly avoided the pain that emanated from acknowledging Jesus during a very difficult time, likely experiencing anxiety about what might happen should he state he was a follower of Jesus.

Above all else, "Jesus pain" (i.e., "clean" pain) can be contrasted with "Peter pain" (i.e., "dirty" pain) in that "Jesus pain" is about pushing forward, following God's plan in spite of the difficulty ahead. With "Jesus pain," to be sure, psychological distress does not go away; still, because Jesus lived his life to be aligned with the will of God, he did not go on to experience "Peter pain." For Peter, he likely experienced both anxiety and uncertainty about what might happen next. He did not know for sure what would happen to Jesus, someone he had faithfully followed for the last few years. He also recognized the pain of denying Jesus during a crucial time, struggling to live out his faith in a bold, vibrant manner. In fact, he denied Jesus in spite of suggesting he would faithfully follow Jesus in Luke 22:33 (i.e., "Lord, I am ready to go with you to prison and to death").

As you consider how to apply this metaphor to your life, remember that you have countless opportunities to convert "Peter pain" into "Jesus pain," surrendering to God's plan from moment to moment. Certainly, Peter went on to radically follow Jesus, despite his three denials. This is a testament to the idea that the Christian life is filled with innumerable chances since God is active and present in the here and now. One way to contemplate the shift from avoidance to acceptance, beyond the Jesus and Peter distinction, involves a concept frequently written about in the ACT literature. This concept will be reviewed next.

Creative Hopelessness with God: Moving from Avoidance to Acceptance

In ACT, *creative hopelessness* is a term that describes the paradigm shift that takes place, moving from avoidance to acceptance (Hayes et al., 2012). To date, attempts to avoid unpleasant thoughts, feelings, and sensations have probably not worked for you, leading to concrete behaviors in the outer world to avoid life. For example, you may be struggling with the symptoms of social anxiety disorder, avoiding the inner experience of anxiety through distraction and substance misuse. Additionally, you might be avoiding social situations, convinced that the answer to social anxiety is staying away from distressing interpersonal interactions, given you feel judged or embarrassed around others.

At a certain point, though, you may have the realization that avoiding both the inner and outer world only leaves you feeling more stuck, exacerbating an already painful situation with the feeling of missing out on life. As you focus on the avoidance of pain, you may spend more time alone, given that public life seems to be intimately linked to anxiety. This aloneness can create added problems, which may be more unbearable than the original symptoms—you might have always longed for deeper relational connections, and may be watching life pass you by as *other people* cultivate satisfying, lasting bonds.

With creative hopelessness, you begin to open up to the possibility that avoiding symptoms does not work, and is responsible for the suffering you are currently going through. The *hopeless* part of the term captures the "rock bottom" feeling you might be having, recognizing that avoidance has an expiration date. Reminiscent of someone who realizes that drinking alcohol has led to an unmanageable life, the hopeless feeling you may be having in this context is a good thing, believe it or not. This feeling can serve as a catalyst towards considering alternative ways to live life, beyond the total eradication of pain, which is often unrealistic and unattainable.

Therefore, the *creative* component of the phrase encompasses all of the possibilities that are now available, since you may be ready to consider different ways to relate to your inner pain. Although you may have previously only *entertained* the idea that making peace with your distress will lead to a livable life, you might now recognize (after reviewing all the avoidance strategies that have not worked and are keeping you on the "sidelines of life") that an alternative approach is the best way forward. With this "light bulb" going off, you are likely ready to shake things up, in a good way.

As a Christian, God is likely a central part of your life. On some level, you probably recognize his active presence in daily living. Still, at times, you may have a hard time seeing him as sovereign, infinitely wise, loving, and good. These attributes, in combination, mean that God is in complete control of your life (even your inner world, filled with distressing thoughts, feelings, and sensations), knows what is best for your life (even when you are not sure), and offers an infinite amount of love, beyond comprehension.

Because of this, creative hopelessness with God involves letting go of the tendency to want to control the inner world, apart from God, recognizing that autonomy and independence have not worked thus far. Rather, surrendering the inner world to God involves sitting at the feet of Jesus, reminiscent of Mary in the gospel of Luke. Embracing a yielding posture of submission, this shift from avoidance to acceptance means surrendering to him, consistent with Alcohol Anonymous' recommendation to "surrender to a higher power." Your prayer, consistent with both creative hopelessness and the Christian faith, might go something like this:

- God, I have tried my best, on my own, to eliminate my pain. I have tried numbing my inner world and avoiding life, among other strategies. Yet, the result has only been added suffering. In fact, I continue to struggle to follow your will for my life, since I am regularly distracted in this tug-of-war. Today, I am letting go of my own efforts to get rid of my distress. Instead, I am trusting in your plan, giving you control over my inner world, surrendering it to you. Whatever your will may be, I am going to trust in you, recognizing that you are infinitely loving, wise, and powerful.

Of course, your actual prayer is likely to be different from the example I provided above. Nevertheless, the purpose is to begin a conversation with God, "transferring the reins" by recognizing that he is in charge. Although the pain might not go away, considering that God is in control of your inner world can bring added peace and comfort, knowing that he has a plan for you. To continue with this shift from avoidance to acceptance, next, you will begin to identify specific avoidance strategies that have distracted you from a life fully devoted to God.

Exercise: Identifying Avoidance Strategies that Keep You Stuck

In this exercise, I would like for you to reflect on all the different concrete ways that you have tried to eliminate your psychological pain, listing out the attempts you have made (in terms of specific behaviors you have relied upon) in the last several years. You might want to consider strategies you have employed to try to numb the pain, such as drug or alcohol use, which may have only made your life worse, exacerbating an already difficult situation. Or, maybe you have tried to distract yourself from the pain through Internet use, including pornography or social networking. As another example, maybe you have isolated yourself from others, cancelling events because of anticipating that something would go wrong. Overall, the purpose of this exercise is to consider the ways that life has become more unmanageable as you have tried to eliminate the pain. Because your efforts have probably come up short, and may have even made life worse, try to consider some of the ways you have tried to cope that are problematic in and of themselves.

1 _____

_____

2 _____

_____

3 _____

_____

4 _____

_____

5 _____

_____

6 _____

_____

7 _____

_____

8 _____

   _____

9 _____

   _____

10 _____

   _____

After completing this exercise, please take a moment to reflect on this list. What do you notice? Are there certain themes, in terms of the actual behaviors you have been using? How, if at all, have these behaviors made your life worse, beyond merely failing to eliminate the pain?

Exercise: Placing Your Avoidance Strategies on the Proverbial Altar[4]

As the above list likely reveals, you have tried quite a few strategies to avoid unpleasant inner experiences, probably coming up well short of your goal of total symptom annihilation. In the meantime, you have possibly devoted a considerable amount of time and energy to eradicating inner pain. In fact, you may be currently feeling hopeless, exhausted, and demoralized, questioning when the pain will end and wondering where God is in this stalled process of healing. One thing is for certain, though—your best efforts at avoidance have likely not worked.

Within ACT, creative hopelessness (as noted above) is a way to make sense of a powerful pivot that needs to take place at this point in the journey. Turning away from avoidance and towards acceptance takes quite a bit of courage, to be sure, but there are also crucial elements of hope and commitment, given that you may be desperately ready to try something new. Stated differently, since avoidance has not tended to work long-term, possibly leaving you feeling glued to *both* the initial symptoms *and* the pain of missing out on life (Hayes, 2005), it might be time for a new strategy, filled with new possibilities.

Within this guided exercise, you will be considering the notion that you can hand over *all* of your avoidance strategies to God, reminiscent of Israel's use of various types of offerings at the Tabernacle altar as a way to fully commit to God, surrendering everything to him. Although there were a plethora of reasons (e.g., guilt, sin, worship, thanksgiving) to offer regular sacrifices to God in the Old Testament (see Leviticus), trusting and hoping in him were central themes within the process, acknowledging total dependence on, and obedience to, God (Boadt, 1984; Wiersbe, 2007). In fact, part of the offering process involved Israel sacrificing its very best to God (Wiersbe, 2007).

To begin this exercise, try to imagine being eagerly ready to offer a sacrifice (your best animal, quite possibly) to God as a way to capture your gratitude towards him, along with your utter dependence and willingness to yield to his will. In other words, you will be offering your sacrifice as a way to let God know you are ready for a new way, hoping to follow Jesus faithfully from this point forward in a vibrant manner. Rather than offering an animal, though, you will be setting all of your *best* avoidance strategies on the altar. Your job, of course, is to completely and totally let go, recognizing that you have given them to God as a way to surrender your life to him, placing your trust and hope in his sovereignty, infinite wisdom, and goodness. As you say goodbye to all of your deeply ingrained avoidance patterns, including your *best* efforts to carry them out, your eyes slowly move towards God, who you now depend on as *the* source of sustenance and survival.

Certainly, this illustration is by no means perfect, likely falling well short of capturing the courage it takes to let go of your avoidance strategies. However, the act of letting go is a central ingredient in this process, shifting from self-reliance to trust in God, reminiscent of the sacrificial system in the Old Testament. To be sure, offering your avoidance strategies to God can serve as a reminder that they do not work, falling short of their lofty goal—the total elimination of pain. To continue with this theme—letting go of avoidance by trusting in God's goodness, wisdom, and power—you will be learning about a way to lament to God, crying out to him, trusting in his responsiveness during periods of intense pain.

Exercise: Cultivating Acceptance by Writing Your Own Lament to God[5]

For this exercise, you will write your own lament to God, using the lament psalms (e.g., Psalm 22) as a model for crying out to God in the midst of psychological pain. Since the psalmists authentically expressed their pain to God, trusting in God even though their suffering did not always go away, try to avoid holding back. If possible, attempt to emphasize the emotional pain you are in, as well as any distressing thoughts (e.g., confusion, doubt) you might have about your current life experiences. The lament can relate to a variety of circumstances, including recurrent inner pain or a recent disappointing event that has left you feeling anxious or depressed.

As noted below, psalmists typically expressed their laments via several different components, including (but not limited to) a complaint to God, a request for God's help, an expression of anger towards God, a positive affirmation directed to God, and some sort of acknowledgement that God has heard the lament (adapted from Brueggemann, 1984).

Complaint to God	
Request for God's Help	
Expression of Anger to God	
Positive Affirmation towards God	
Acknowledgment that God Has Heard the Lament	

Once you have finished, please try to reflect on the exercise. What was it like to cry out to God, articulating the pain you are in? How, if at all, is your lament different from some of the avoidance strategies you have historically used? How can you use additional laments to reach out to God, inviting him into the process to accept (rather than avoid) psychological pain, reminiscent of the psalmists?

Conclusion

In this chapter, you explored experiential avoidance in general, as well as some of its specific ingredients, relating the dilemma of avoidance to emotional disorders. In addition, you read about different examples of avoidance in the Bible, as well as desert Christians' view on the topic. To stay in the "cell," which can represent psychological and spiritual functioning in the inner world, means to depend totally on God, given that he is there with you in the mist of your pain. Rather than running from the "cell," "staying put" means that a move from avoidance to acceptance needs to take place.

Within the ACT literature, creative hopelessness encompasses this type of a paradigm shift, recognizing that all of your avoidance strategies, to date, have failed to deliver on the promise of total pain eradication. As a Christian, creative hopelessness involves recognizing that your efforts to eliminate the pain may have historically gotten in the way of following Jesus. As a result, acceptance (which is not, by any means, the same thing as agreement) may be a useful alternative, especially if your purpose on this planet is to follow Jesus. Ultimately, maintaining a permanent sense of happiness may be an impossible aim, given it is an extremely difficult emotion to define, let alone capture and pin down.

To place your prior avoidance strategies "on the altar" before God means there is a willingness to let go, trusting that God is in command. Finally, lamenting to God can help you cry out to him when you are in pain, relying on his safety, comfort, and nourishment, rather than self-derived avoidance strategies. In the next chapter, you will begin to explore, in much more detail, the six processes of ACT, aligning them with the Christian tradition.

Notes

1 For a succinct, yet informative, summary of the "cell," see Chryssavgis (2008).

2 The quotes in this section are from Wortley (2012). Used with permission.

3 This metaphor is influenced by Wilson and DuFrene's (2010) example of Peter's struggle to live out his faith in the gospel accounts.

4 Worth mentioning, this exercise is only meant to serve as a metaphor for surrendering to God, rather than to suggest in any way that the sacrificial system mentioned in Exodus is an effective means to secure God's forgiveness in the 21st century. To be sure, in the New Testament, Hebrews clearly articulates that Jesus is now the "great high priest," who provides "purification for sins."

5 This exercise is influenced by the lament intervention in Dworsky, Pargament, Gibbel, Krumrei, Faigin, Haugen, Desai, Lauricella, Lynn, and Warner (2013).

References

Boadt, L. (1984). *Reading the Old Testament: An Introduction.* New York: Paulist Press.

Brueggemann, W. (1984). *The Message of the Psalms: A Theological Commentary.* Minneapolis, MN: Augsburg Publishing House.

Chryssavgis, J. (2008). *In The Heart of The Desert: the Spirituality of the Desert Fathers and Mothers.* Bloomington, IN: World Wisdom, Inc.

Gamez, W., Chmielewski, M., Kotov, R., Ruggero, C., & Watson, D. (2011). Development of a Measure of Experiential Avoidance: The Multidimensional Experiential Avoidance Questionnaire. *Psychological Assessment, 23,* 692–713.

Hayes, S. (2005). *Get Out of Your Mind and Into Your Life: The New Acceptance & Commitment Therapy.* Oakland, CA: New Harbinger Publications, Inc.

Hayes, S., Strosahl, K., & Wilson, K. (1999). *Acceptance and Commitment Therapy: An Experiential Approach to Behavioral Change.* New York: The Guilford Press.

Hayes, S., Strosahl, K., & Wilson, K. (2012). *Acceptance and Commitment Therapy: The Process and Practice of Mindful Change* (2nd ed.). New York: The Guilford Press.

Knabb, J., & Grigorian-Routon, A. (2014). The role of experiential avoidance in the relationship between faith maturity, religious coping, and psychological adjustment among Christian university students. *Mental Health, Religion & Culture, 17,* 458–469.

Oemig, C., Pargament, K., Gibbel, M., Krumrei, E., Faigin, C., Haugen, M., Desai, K., Lauricella, S., Lynn, Q., & Warner, H. (2013). Winding road: Preliminary support for a spiritually integrated intervention addressing college students' spiritual struggles. *Research in the Social Scientific Study of Religion, 24,* 309–339.

Wiersbe, W. (2007). *The Wiersbe Bible Commentary: Old Testament.* Colorado Springs, CO: David C. Cook.

Wilson, K., & DuFrene, T. (2010). *Things Might Go Terribly, Horribly Wrong: A Guide to Life Liberated from Anxiety.* Oakland, CA: New Harbinger Publications, Inc.

Wortley, J. (2012). *The Book of Elders: Sayings of the Desert Fathers.* Trappist, KY: Cistercian Publications.

Chapter 3: Cognitive Defusion and Watchfulness with Thinking

Introduction
In this chapter, you will learn about ACT's defusion process, which can help you begin to notice your thinking patterns with a bit more distance, flexibility, and openness, similar to watching a tumbleweed blow down your street from the window of your house. Moreover, you will learn about a similar strategy, watchfulness, utilized by early desert Christians to observe tempting, compulsive thoughts with a calm vigilance. Using the Jesus Prayer, you will practice the ability to notice gently your thoughts run their natural course, without getting bullied around by them, something with which you may have historically struggled. Because cognitive fusion (the opposite of defusion) can get in the way of value-based living, ACT emphasizes learning new strategies to relate to thoughts with more tentativeness and distance. Finally, you will learn about several defusion/watchfulness metaphors in order to view thinking a bit differently, practicing several exercises to help you relate to your cognitive processes with more openness and flexibility.

ACT and Cognitive Defusion
Within ACT, cognitive fusion involves being pushed around by thinking, automatically assuming that the mind generates accurate, factual, and objective information (Hayes, Strosahl, & Wilson, 2012). When you are fused with your thinking, there is no other reality—thoughts are facts. This relationship to the mind, of course, can quickly become problematic when you assume all of your thoughts are true, given that the mind can be notoriously unreliable, especially when attempting to live out your values. For example, you might think to yourself, "I'm inherently unlikable and flawed," which can get in the way of your value of deepening intimate relationships, loving others like Jesus loved those with whom he came into contact.

In a state of fusion, it is almost as if the mind is an Encyclopedia Britannica, which an elementary school student automatically assumes contains accurate, factual information, given that the material is in printed form. Similar to opening an encyclopedia, almost robotically trusting the words on the page are objective and true, fusion involves trusting the mind's ability to generate language to make sense of both the inner (e.g., thoughts, feelings, sensations) and outer (e.g., relationships, events) world.

On the other hand, in a state of defusion, you are able to relate to your thoughts with much less certainty, recognizing that the words your mind has generated might or might not be true (Hayes et al., 2012). With defusion, the mind is more like an Internet blog—merely a medium for communicating information, sometimes exaggerated and opinion based. To be sure, in the 21st century, you would never assume information is accurate just because you have found it on the Internet among a sea of bloggers.

In a state of cognitive fusion, your mind may generate several patterns of thinking that can get in the way of living out your values. Such patterns include rigid views about yourself, your past, or future; judgmental thinking about yourself or others; reasons for a lack of value-based action; and indisputable rules (adapted from Harris, 2009):

- Describing yourself negatively, often in black-and-white ways.

  - "I'm useless."
  - "I'm worthless."
  - "I'm undeserving of love."

- Reliving the past or catastrophizing about a yet-to-be-determined future.

  - "I can't believe I said that to him—I'm so embarrassed and can't move on."
  - "There is no way I'll be able to succeed tomorrow."
  - "I know I'll fail at the job interview next week."

- Judging yourself or others, typically with overgeneralizations or dichotomous thinking.

  - "He's a complete failure."
  - "I'm a loser."
  - "There is no way someone would ever love me because of my past."

- Reasoning your way out of value-based action.

  - "I'm stuck with depression and must isolate myself—after all, it's a genetic predisposition."
  - "Next year, I will do a better job living out my values."
  - "I can't date right now because I'm too anxious."

- Relying on rules to determine a course of action.

  - "I can't go to the party because I'm too depressed."
  - "I can't ask her out to lunch because I'm way too socially anxious."
  - "Because I might have a panic attack, I definitely can't lead the small group ministry at my church."

From an ACT perspective, the most problematic part of fusion is that overly relying on the mind can get in the way of value-based action. For example, you may have a New Year's resolution about exercising, which is linked to the value of maintaining your health. Come January 1st, you might wake up in the morning with a mind that tells you it is too early to get out of bed. Or, your mind might tell you that it is too crowded at the gym, so why bother. As another potential barrier, your mind might convince you that signing up at the gym is a great idea—for next month. When your mind begins to generate letters in the alphabet, which form words carefully strung together in sentences, the world of language can quickly begin to dominate your behavior.

Conversely, your values will lead you down a very different path, and can offer a much more reliable map to guide life. If you have always valued physical health, your mind can easily serve as a barrier to healthy living. As this example reveals, on January 1st, your mind wants to take you down a different road than your values. When this happens, defusion can help you to bring your mind along for the ride, so to speak, recognizing that your mind will continue to generate these kinds of statements, which are sometimes inaccurate.

It is almost as if the mind is like a team of advisers to the President of the United States. At times, the President's advisers will agree with one another, offering the President a unified strategy for responding to a crisis. At other times, they will be in disagreement, with some advisers offering better suggestions than others. For the President, the purpose of advisers is to receive a range of perspectives, ultimately choosing what is best for the country. Certainly, the President needs to cross-reference these incoming opinions with a set of pre-determined principles, which are deeply ingrained in the heart.

This metaphor can be applied to the inner world of language, given that the mind can sometimes be helpful, sending you down the road of value-based living, reminiscent of presidential advisers that offer sound advice, advancing an agenda that is best for the country. Still, advisers are in no way perfect; thus, at times, they will inevitably have a bad day, struggling to come up with solutions that will benefit the citizens of the United States. Because of this, your job is to recognize that the mind has good days and bad days, letting the mind do its job—generate thoughts.

To cultivate a state of defusion, recognizing that the mind is not the "be-all, end-all" of the decision-making process, ACT utilizes a range of metaphors, techniques, and exercises. For example, ACT tends to metaphorically "externalize the mind" (Hayes et al., 2012) in order to create some distance between your sense of self and your thinking patterns. Therefore, the mind might be viewed in the following ways:

- The mind is like a heckling fan in the stadium.

    ○ If you are an athlete performing in front of a crowd, you can allow the heckling fan to say whatever he wants, focusing on the task at hand in spite of the disruption; after all, major league baseball will always have fans in the stadium, watching and evaluating the game.

- The mind is like an annoying commercial.

    ○ When you are watching television, the same annoying commercial comes on, over and over again, which you can just chuckle at, rather than allow it to ruin the show you are watching; because network television will continue to have commercials for funding, they will always be present in some way, shape, or form.

- The mind is like a loud neighbor in an apartment complex.

    ○ You have lived in several different apartment complexes, always seeming to get stuck next to a loud neighbor; because of the nature of apartment living—people live in close proximity to one another, and not everyone is overly considerate—you are able to allow your neighbor to live his or her life, recognizing that you don't need to get worked up about the scenario.

- The mind is like a rude uncle at the Thanksgiving dinner table.

  ○ Every Thanksgiving, you have to interact with your rude uncle, recognizing that you can enjoy your conversations with others at the dinner table, accepting that your uncle struggles to understand social etiquette; after all, he is a member of the family, too.

Notice that each of these metaphors can help you recognize that the mind is not always accurate, helpful, or supportive, and does not ultimately need to determine the direction you take in life. You can still live out your values, accepting that your mind is going to come along for the journey.

Also, ACT encourages you to place "I'm having the thought that …" before your actual thoughts (Harris, 2009). For example, instead of thinking to yourself, "I am ugly," you would state, "I'm having the thought that 'I'm ugly.'" Of course, the difference is that you are acknowledging the "I'm ugly" thought is just a thought, practicing the ability to defuse from the thinking process.

Finally, ACT utilizes guided meditations to practice defusing from the thinking process. As a classic exercise, "Leaves on the Stream" (Harris, 2009; Hayes et al., 2012) involves envisioning that you are sitting on the bank of a stream, beneath a tree that extends out over the water. As you watch the stream, you notice that the leaves are falling gently into the water. When they hit the water, they float lightly down the stream. Your job is to notice each time your mind generates a thought, writing the thought on each leaf as it floats down to the water. In this exercise, you are paying particular attention to your ability to watch your thoughts, simply letting them fall with the leaves as they float down the stream. The purpose, of course, is not to push away your thinking, but to recognize that you can watch your thoughts with an open curiosity, similar to the way you may tend to view nature with a sense of mystery and awe.

Overall, defusion exercises are intended to help you relate to your thinking mind with a bit more tentativeness, openness, curiosity, and distance, rather than assuming your mind is generating accurate statements that *must* be followed at all costs. By defusing, you can flexibly respond to environmental demands (as well as inner experiences) with value-based living, choosing the direction you would like to take in life, rather than being bullied around by the mind. Instead of running a three-legged race, with the mind as your partner, who is dragging you away from the finish line, you are running *your* race, watching other runners compete out of the corner of your eye, without feeling forced to head in *their* chosen direction.

Interestingly, early desert Christians developed their own way to observe the inner workings of the mind with more distance and flexibility. What follows is a review of their approach to interacting with the thinking mind. This approach involves a calm vigilance, noticing distracting, tempting, and compulsive thoughts that can get in the way of virtuous living, deepening an awareness of God's loving presence. After this discussion, you will learn about the Jesus Prayer, which is a specific way to practice watchfulness in the Christian tradition.

Early Desert Christians and Watchfulness

Among the early desert Christians, *watchfulness* (the Greek word, *nepsis*) involves being aware of the inner world, including thoughts, as well as recognizing God's active, loving, responsive presence (Burton-Christie, 1993). For Evagrius, a 4th-century monk, watchfulness involved being aware of compulsive, tempting thoughts (the Greek word, *logismoi*) surrounding eight distinct themes (adapted from Harmless, 2008):

- Greed
- Sex
- Gluttony
- Sadness
- Anger
- Restlessness
- Pride
- Vanity

Overall, being attentive to the inner workings of the mind, recognizing when tempting, compulsive thoughts pull you away from God, is key in the Christian life, especially among contemplatives throughout the ages.

For the early desert Christians, watchfulness was developed within the "cell," a room that they lived in, wherein they focused on prayer, simple tasks (e.g., basket weaving), and reciting scripture. Within the confines of the cell, focusing on a prayer word helped them to get to know the patterns of the inner world, maintaining a vigilant awareness of wavering intrapsychic experiences (Lane, 1998). Eventually, reciting prayers developed into the Jesus Prayer sometime later, "Lord Jesus Christ, Son of God, have mercy on me, a sinner," which is outlined in the next section.

Nevertheless, examples of watchfulness from the *Sayings of the Desert Fathers*[1] are as follows:

- "Prison means staying soberly in the cell, ever mindful of God."
- "A monk ought to be all eyes, like the cherubim and the seraphim."
- "If we keep up our practice and are attentively vigilant, we shall not find any defilement in ourselves."
- "Just as the soldiers of the emperor standing before him dare not turn their attention to the left or to the right, so nothing of the enemy can frighten the person standing before God and being in fear of him all the time."
- "We are taken prisoner by the passions of the flesh because of our lack of mental attention in our contemplation of God."
- "Whether you are sleeping or waking up or doing something else, if God is before your eyes, the enemy can in no way make you afraid. If this [thought] remains within a person, the power of God remains with him too."

Notice, here, that the focus is on being aware of the distractions of the inner world so as to avoid getting pulled away from your focus on God's presence.[2] Given that residing in the "cell" meant that monks had to face the inner world, they had to learn a new way to respond to tempting, compulsive thoughts that distracted them from a deeper union with God. Their surefire way to cultivate vigilance was to shift their focus repeatedly to God's presence.

Watchfulness, of course, parallels ACT's defusion process in that both are focused on relating differently to thoughts, recognizing the patterns of the mind with a bit more distance. By doing this, you can pivot towards the central goal in life for Christians—following Jesus. Rather than being preoccupied with a variety of thought patterns, staying stuck in the process, watchfulness is a way to notice gently when the mind has shifted, rededicating yourself to an awareness of God's presence. What follows is an introduction to the Jesus Prayer, which can help you to focus your attention when you notice you are being swept away by the stream of the mind, distracted from following Jesus in daily living.

The Jesus Prayer: An Introduction[3]
For early desert Christians, reciting scripture was employed as a way to focus their attention on God, especially while in the "cell," wherein they could be tempted with compulsive thoughts that distracted

them. Over time, reciting scripture (often the Psalms) led to the Jesus Prayer: "Lord Jesus Christ, Son of God, have mercy on me, a sinner." This prayer may have come from some of the examples in the gospels of people asking Jesus for mercy and confessing sin.

In the 21st century, the Jesus Prayer is especially popular in the Greek Orthodox Church, cultivating watchfulness through the use of this famous saying. Within the practice, which can be employed both formally and informally, Christians recite the prayer over and over again in rhythm with their breathing. With the in-breath, "Lord Jesus Christ, Son of God," is recited. Next, with the out-breath, "Have mercy on me, a sinner," is gently exhaled. Within the practice, which can be completed formally in 20-minute blocks of time and informally throughout the day, the mind is focused on Jesus, rather than distracting, compulsive thoughts that get in the way of being fully attentive to him.

Over time, the Jesus Prayer can help to cultivate sustained attention, focusing entirely on God's presence. As you repeatedly shift from your distracting thoughts to God's presence, you can notice the fluctuating patterns of the mind, recognizing that your thoughts do not need to dominate your experience of God. Again, the repetition of the prayer—which is recited in the heart, rather than repeated as a merely cognitive endeavor—helps to focus your attention on God, praying with a sense of consistency, commitment, and dedication.

In a subsequent section of this chapter, you will have the opportunity to practice the Jesus Prayer. Until then, I would like to review watchfulness in the Bible, along with my interpretation of the link between watchfulness, the Mary mode (from the Gospel of Luke), and contemplation. From there, you will apply watchfulness to emotional disorders, before beginning several exercises to cultivate a defused, watchful state. Remember, the main point of watchfulness is to maintain an awareness of distracting, fused thinking, which can pull you away from being alert to God's active, loving presence.

Watchfulness in the Bible

Perhaps the most famous passage that contemplative authors point to in order to capture watchfulness, 1 Peter 5:8–9 emphasizes the salience of being alert and focused in the Christian life:

- "Be alert and of sober mind. Your enemy the devil prowls around like a roaring lion looking for someone to devour. Resist him, standing firm in the faith, because you know that the family of believers through the world is undergoing the same kind of sufferings."

Here, you will see that Peter instructed Christians to be sober, alert, and mindful. To remain watchful, to be sure, involves a high degree of attentiveness, especially due to the consequences of "falling asleep at the wheel," so to speak. For Christians, the devil is a "roaring lion," consistent with Evagrius' view that compulsive, tempting thoughts can get in the way of an awareness of God's loving presence and total devotion to him.

As one more example, in Matthew 24:42–44, Jesus expressed the importance of being watchful and vigilant in the context of Jesus' eventual return:

- "Therefore, keep watch because you do not know on what day your Lord will come. But understand this: If the owner of the house had known at what time of night the thief was coming, he would have kept watch and would not have let his house be broken into. So you must be ready because the Son of Man will come at an hour when you do not expect him."

Again, within this passage, there is an emphasis on a sort of sober, vigilant, attentive watchfulness, remaining alert to God's presence. Rather than being swept away by compulsive, tempting thoughts, Christians are advised to remain aware and "wide-eyed" for Jesus' inevitable return.

In the context of emotional disorders, fused thinking can become a distraction to following Jesus. Given that you do not know the exact date and time that Jesus will return, applying a sober attentiveness to the inner world means getting to know the mind, including its tendency to distract and block you from following Jesus, especially with regard to depressive and anxiety-related thoughts.

For example, you might firmly believe that you are "worthless," as well as "useless" when it comes to serving in your church and following Jesus. Moreover, you may be preoccupied with perceived future catastrophes, anticipating that something will go terribly wrong in the near or distant future. When you become fused with these compulsive types of thinking patterns, which seem very factual at the time, you may end up avoiding life.

As both Peter and Jesus noted, an attentive vigilance means remaining watchful, noticing when you have been hijacked by the mind, reminiscent of a terrorist taking over an airplane. When this happens, you (the pilot) are no longer determining the course of the flight, consistent with a fused state, allowing your thoughts to hijack your valued living. Before going into more detail about the relationship between watchfulness and emotional disorders, I would like to spend a little time unpacking the relationship between watchfulness and the Mary mode, reminiscent of the "being" mode in mindfulness practice.

Watchfulness and the Mary Mode

With the Mary mode (i.e., Mary sitting at Jesus' feet in Luke's gospel), you are able to sit simply at the feet of Jesus, letting go of all efforts to change, fix, clutch, or avoid the inner world. Because you are sitting at Jesus' feet, there is nowhere else to be and absolutely nothing else to do. In other words, you are surrendering to God's providence. Instead of frantically running around, striving compulsively to manage your inner world, reminiscent of Martha in the gospel of Luke, your job is to listen humbly to Jesus.

To relate the Mary mode to watchfulness, when you are sitting at Jesus' feet, you can relate to your thinking with a bit more flexibility and distance, letting your thoughts play out their natural course, without investing in them in any way. As you gaze upon Jesus, submitting to his will, you are letting go of the tendency to use your thinking patterns to guide what you are doing. Watchfulness in the Mary mode, therefore, involves acknowledging your thoughts, before gently returning to the task at hand—sitting at Jesus' feet in a restful state of contemplation.

Overall, watchfulness at Jesus' feet involves a single point of focus—Jesus—along with the recognition that you are firmly rooted in the present moment, letting go of the tendency to chase ruminative or worrying thoughts in the past or future. When you notice that Martha is scurrying about, anxiously driven and task oriented, you can simply acknowledge her presence. This story in Luke, of course, is reminiscent of an overreliance on the thinking mind—shifting from Martha to Mary's style can help you to return gently to your loving gaze, recognizing that letting go of all activity is key when you are at his feet. Certainly, there will be instances when Martha's style is necessary, especially when living out virtue-based action; yet, when it comes to the inner world, Mary's mode is optimal.

Of course, watchfulness and the Mary mode are similar to defusion, the "being" mode (Williams, 2008), and mindfulness, given that you are letting your thoughts do what they are going to do, without striving to change them in any way. Rather, you are essentially saying to God, "I am surrendering my thoughts to you. Please do with them what you wish. During this time, I don't want to rely on my mind. Instead, I want to rest in your presence, trusting in your providence."

Watchfulness and Emotional Disorders

To apply watchfulness to emotional disorders, you will practice simply noticing your compulsive, tempting thoughts, reminiscent of the early desert Christians' ability to observe the *logismoi* in their cell. Rather than running from their tempting thoughts, or allowing them to determine monks' course of action, these early Christians faced them in order to recognize them. However, in the process, they also realized that their thoughts were not always helpful in pursuing virtuous living.

Instead of focusing on the eight distinct *logismoi* (i.e., tempting thoughts), with emotional disorders, you are acknowledging certain types of thoughts that get in the way of action-based living. Thus, in the space that follows, please write down your top five compulsive, tempting thoughts that have historically gotten in the way of following Jesus. These thoughts may be organized around your self-concept, the past or future, judgments, reasons, or rules (Harris, 2009), and may be linked to other depressive or anxiety-related symptoms. For example, you might recognize the thought, "I'm worthless," or that you have been overly fused with a past conversation, which leads to social isolation. Or, you might be predicting something will go wrong in the future, exacerbating your anxiety. Finally, you may judge your depressive symptoms as "bad," or offer reasons or rules for why you will have to wait for your symptoms to go away to live life (e.g., "I'll follow Jesus when the depression goes away").

1 _____

_____

2 _____

_____

3 _____

_____

4 _____

_____

5 _____

_____

Watchfulness Metaphors

Within ACT, there are a variety of metaphors used to capture a state of cognitive defusion. In a state of defusion, thoughts are experienced much more tentatively, rather than assumed to be true, factual, or entirely accurate. Similarly, with watchfulness, you can observe the inner workings of the mind, recognizing when your mind is generating distracting, compulsive thoughts that can get in the way of following Jesus.

Below are a few watchfulness metaphors to help you relate to your thoughts with less certainty, letting go of the tendency to compulsively act on them when they seem like they are the "truth" for your life. In a state of watchful defusion, your relationship to your thoughts is as follows:

- Your thoughts are like the waves on the Sea of Galilee. Since you are in the boat with Jesus, you can safely watch them, recognizing that God is in control.

- Your thoughts are like judgmental Pharisees, constantly stopping you to question your motives as you travel with Jesus as one of his disciples. Since you are with Jesus, you can confidently continue, recognizing that the Pharisees will not get in the way of your mission. Watching the Pharisees, you recognize their arguments are extremely short-sighted, given you are with your Lord and Savior.

- Your thoughts are reminiscent of the devil tempting Jesus in the wilderness. Although the devil promised Jesus the world, Jesus confidently responded with God's word, recognizing that he had a mission to accomplish. In fact, Jesus was alert and sober in his ability to focus on scripture, rather than lofty promises from the devil.

- Your thoughts are like the clever serpent in the Garden of Eden, trying to convince you to be like God, rather than dependent on God. Because of this, you can simply decline to eat the forbidden fruit, returning to your dependence on God, trusting in his providential care. To remain watchful, you can maintain alertness, recognizing whenever the serpent is using his clever, crafty arguments to convince you to turn away from God.

- Your thoughts are like some of Jesus' disciples, with a doubting Thomas, denying Peter, and betraying Judas. When you notice your mind is engaging in these types of tactics—which is to be expected, given that you are a human being—you can acknowledge you have drifted (like Jesus' disciples), before returning to your task at hand.

- Your thoughts are like some of the Israelites who wanted to turn around and head back to Egypt, struggling to follow Moses in the desert to the "promised land." Remaining watchful involves recognizing that these fellow travelers may continue to grumble, but that you are focused on following Moses (and God, more importantly) to your final destination.

Certainly, you can come up with your own biblical metaphors for embracing a watchful, defused state when relating to your thoughts. Remember, the most important part of this type of sober vigilance with your thinking is that you are recognizing when your cognitions are getting in the way of following Jesus.

Exercise: Eating from the Tree of Knowledge of Good and Evil[4]
For this exercise, you will simply try to notice the thoughts that arise in your mind, gently labeling them when you recognize that your mind is eating from the "tree of the knowledge of good and evil," independent of God's will. Like Adam and Eve partaking of this forbidden tree in the Garden of Eden (see Genesis 2–3), because of the fall, Christians can sometimes struggle with trying to be like God in knowing good and evil, attempting to judge inner experiences apart from God's omniscience. Of course, judging is very different from *discerning*, which involves understanding God's will via prayer, studying scripture, and mature Christian relationships.

With this guided meditation, you will simply notice your mind's tendency to eat from this outlawed tree, labeling your thoughts (e.g., "judging") when they arise. In turn, you will gently allow these lingering thoughts to run their natural course, without "biting into" them and tasting them, reminiscent of just noticing the forbidden tree in the garden without actually eating the fruit. If possible, with your eyes closed, try to do this exercise for about twenty minutes in a quiet environment, sitting upright in a comfortable position. After you are done, try to write down some of the judgmental thoughts that you noticed, and reflect on your experience of the exercise.

Some possible questions to consider for reflection: (a) what types of judgmental thoughts arose during the exercise? (b) were you able to allow them to simply be, without actually entertaining them by eating the forbidden fruit? (c) in daily life, how well are you able to simply allow these types of judgmental thoughts to run their natural course, without taking a bite out of them? and (d) how might you remind yourself throughout the day to let go of the tendency to listen to the serpent in the proverbial garden, biting into the very fruit that leads to trying to be like God, judging both inner and outer events, independent of his will?

_____

_____

_____

_____

_____

_____

_____

Exercise: Identifying Judgmental, Pharisaic Thoughts[5]

In the gospels, the Pharisees seemed to question Jesus constantly, apparently focusing on the letter of the law, rather than the spirit of the law. As a result, they appeared to come across as very black-and-white in their view of people, which Jesus criticized as too legalistic. Of course, the human mind can slip into this mode from time to time, believing it has the monopoly on truth, struggling to let go of a rigid system to guide life (rather than following Jesus, cultivating a relationship with him). When this happens, it can be helpful to examine your thought patterns, especially if you find yourself engaging in dichotomous, Pharisaic thinking, leaving you struggling to follow Jesus, loving others based on the grace and mercy that God has offered to you.

For this exercise, see if you can "externalize the mind," consistent with ACT, by noticing when your mind is being a "Pharisee," overly judging and evaluating at the expense of offering love, mercy, and grace to yourself and others. This type of thinking, which may involve judgments about yourself or others or rigid rules you *have* to follow, can be especially problematic surrounding emotional disorders. In this exercise, just try to notice when your mind is being pharisaic, gently acknowledging your mind's tendencies. There is nothing else to do in this exercise, other than simply recognizing your mind's evaluative nature, offering yourself grace in the process. When you are finished, try to write down some of the thoughts that you noticed, and continue to practice this exercise throughout your day.

_____

_____

_____

_____

_____

_____

_____

_____

Exercise: Leaning on God's Understanding

Within the Christian tradition, Proverbs 3:1–8 is a rather popular section of scripture, capturing the importance of trusting in God, rather than purely human wisdom, which is divorced from him:

- "My son, do not forget my teaching, but keep my commands in your heart, for they will prolong your life many years and bring you peace and prosperity. Let love and faithfulness never leave you; bind them around your neck, write them on the tablet of your heart. Then you will win favor and a good name in the sight of God and man. *Trust in the Lord with all your heart and lean not on your own understanding; in all your ways submit to him, and he will make your paths straight* [italics added]. Do not be wise in your own eyes; fear the Lord and shun evil. This will bring health to your body and nourishment to your bones."

In this exercise, I would like for you to place the phrase, "I will not lean on my own understanding that ..." before some of the depressive or anxiety-related thoughts you notice you have fused with throughout your day. For example, if you think to yourself, "I'm worthless," you would say to yourself, "I will not lean on my own understanding that 'I'm worthless.'" In sum, the purpose of this exercise is to defuse from thinking patterns that keep you stuck, cultivating an attitude of watchfulness and inner vigilance. In turn, letting go of your own understanding, shedding the tendency to employ your own interpretations, can help you pivot towards surrendering to God's plan as you walk with Jesus.

Exercise: The Jesus Prayer[6]

In this exercise, you will be formally practicing the Jesus Prayer in a 20-minute block of time, cultivating a defused watchfulness. Remember to practice in a quiet environment, sitting up straight in a chair that provides support and comfort. Try to practice with your eyes closed, envisioning that you are repeating the prayer in your heart, rather than as a sort of mantra. Really try to sink into the words, recognizing their salience for your life.

Above all else, the practice is designed to help you to acknowledge Jesus as your Lord, as well as surrender to him, asking him for his compassion and mercy. Along the way, you are trying to develop the habit of watchfulness, given that you will be practicing returning gently to the phrase as your mind drifts towards something else.

Below is a sample transcript to get you started with the practice, although you will likely be able to complete the 20-minute exercise on your own after you have read through the below instructions a few times:

- Please get into a comfortable position, sitting up straight with your eyes closed. Say a brief prayer to God, letting him know that you want to surrender your inner world to him, asking for him to have compassion on you as you recite the words of the prayer. Now, when you are ready, begin to slowly and gently recite the Jesus Prayer: "Lord Jesus Christ, Son of God, have mercy on me, a sinner." As you slowly and gently breathe in, inhale, "Lord Jesus Christ, Son of God," acknowledging he is the Lord of your life and God's one and only Son. As you exhale, say, "Have mercy on me, a sinner," asking God to extend his mercy, grace, and compassion to you as you surrender your inner world to him.

- Continue with this exercise, inhaling the first part, followed by exhaling the second part. Again, try to allow the prayer to marinate, resonating deep in your heart. Practice patience with the exercise, too, just allowing the phrase to begin to repeat itself. When you notice your mind has drifted to a different thought, just acknowledge that this has happened with non-judgmental compassion, gently returning to the prayer. Each time you notice your mind has wandered, you are practicing watchfulness, recognizing the patterns of the mind. Try to view these distractions as an amazing opportunity to refocus your attention on Jesus, which is a tremendous gift that is available in each passing moment.
- As the exercise comes to a close, say a prayer to God, thanking him for the opportunity to focus on him, reminiscent of Mary sitting at Jesus' feet, with nothing else to do and nowhere else to be. See if you can continue on with the practice throughout your day, praying the Jesus Prayer whenever you recognize your mind has drifted towards something else, especially a fused state that gets in the way of following Christ.

In the space that follows, see if you can write about your experience, documenting whatever came up in the task. For example, if you noticed you were distracted, what types of thoughts seemed to pull you away from the prayer? What was it like to refocus on Jesus each time you recognized your attention had shifted? How, if at all, can the practice help you throughout your day, especially in the context of fused thinking surrounding emotional disorders?

_____

_____

_____

_____

_____

_____

_____

_____

_____

_____

Exercise: Surrendering Your Lamp to God

To continue developing the ability to be watchful with your think-ing, this exercise will help you to defuse from your thoughts, giving them over to God. The purpose, though, is not to rid yourself of your thoughts; instead, the primary goal of the exercise is to let go of your tendency to rely on your thoughts, depending instead on God's will to guide daily living. Before starting the exercise, I would like for you to read Psalm 119:105–112 in order to reflect on the importance of God's word serving as a "lamp" for the paths of life:

- "Your word is a lamp for my feet, a light on my path. I have taken an oath and confirmed it, that I will follow your righteous laws. I have suffered much; preserve my life, Lord, according to your word. Accept, Lord, the willing praise of my mouth, and teach me your laws. Though I constantly take my life in my hands, I will not forget your law. The wicked have set a snare for me, but I have not strayed from your precepts. Your statutes are my heritage for-ever; they are the joy of my heart. My heart is set on keeping your decrees to the very end."

Now, when you are ready, get into a comfortable position, closing your eyes and sitting up straight in a comfortable chair. Begin to imagine that your thoughts are like your own lamp, guiding your life. To date, you have been heading in the direction that your very own personal lamp has illuminated. Yet, God offers a different lamp. His lamp is perfect, given that it is consistent with his will, and differs from your lamp. Because of this, you have a decision to make—continue to use your own lamp to guide your life (consistent with your own fused thinking habits), or set down your personal lamp in order to pick up God's lamp for guidance along the paths of life (captured in walking faithfully behind Jesus, relying on his teachings).

If possible, try to envision actually letting go of your own lamp, which, again, represents all of your fused, compulsive thoughts that have guided your path thus far in life. These may be the "I'm worth-less" lamp, or the "I'm useless" lamp. Or, you might have to let go of the "I can't follow Jesus because of my anxiety" lamp. Over time, these proverbial lamps have allowed you to make sense of life, but possibly at the expense of following God's plan, reminiscent of his lamp for the path he would like you to travel down.

Of course, the goal is to be guided by God's lamp, which consists of a relationship with Jesus Christ, cross-referenced with the Bible as God's word. Along God's path, illuminated by his lamp, you will continue to find there are lamp stores that offer the newest, best lamp, which will seemingly (though not actually) lead to the permanent path of "happiness" and "pleasure." Whenever you recognize you have walked into a lamp store, maybe even purchasing your own lamp again with the hope of a fixed state of "happiness," remember that you always have the opportunity to simply set down this newly purchased lamp, wherever you are on the path, and pick up God's lamp for guidance.

Above all else, this exercise can help you to recognize the decision you have from moment to moment—rely on your own fused thinking, reminiscent of your own lamp, or turn to God's active presence, leading the way based on his perfect lamp. Consistent with ACT, though, this decision needs to be freely chosen, rather than coercive in any way. In other words, *you* get to make the decision about relying on your own fused thinking or surrendering your thoughts to God in an effort to radically and authentically follow Jesus, even while in psychological pain. After all, God's path, illuminated by his lamp, does not always lead solely to happiness and pleasure (Jesus' life is a perfect example); yet, psychological and spiritual growth can take place along God's road to becoming more like Christ.

When you are finished, see if you can write down some of your reactions to this exercise. What might it be like in your own life to set down your personal lamp, picking up God's lamp for you instead? What types of personal lamps, historically, have you carried, convinced they are the best way to guide you on a path forward? What might be different in your life if you relied less on your own lamp, and more on God's lamp, trusting in him to guide the way, even when your fused thinking seems to be accurate, factual, and settled?

_____

_____

_____

_____

_____

_____

_____

Exercise: Watching Your Thoughts with Jesus

In this chapter's final exercise, I would like for you to imagine that you are sitting with Jesus on a hillside by the Sea of Galilee. As you sit with him, you can feel the wind on your face, and smell the sea in the distance, with the sun shining on a bright, clear day. In this time spent with Jesus, your job is to simply watch the birds as they land on the hillside, search for food, and fly away. In fact, there are quite a few birds lingering around. As you see a bird land, simply imagine your thoughts are like the bird, watching the bird do what it will do, given that God is ultimately in control. Rather than trying to control the bird in any way, just notice what is happening, allowing the bird to symbolize all of the thoughts that arise, linger, and pass away in your mind. Again, there is nothing else to do, other than just watch the birds landing, searching for food, and flying away as you spend time with Jesus.

If possible, try to recognize that God's providence is guiding the birds, especially as they look for food and decide which direction to take to eat each day. To draw a parallel, see if you can let go of the tendency to control your thoughts in any way, surrendering them to God's providence, consistent with the birds you are watching with Jesus. After all, God provides for the birds flying in the air, and clothes the lilies blowing on the hillside (see Matthew 6). If you can, continue on with this exercise for about 10 minutes, gently noticing the birds (i.e., your thoughts) do what they will, reminding your-self that God is in control. Because God is sovereign and infinitely wise and good, you can let God do what he will with your thought processes.

When you are finished with this exercise, try to write down some of the thoughts that emerged. Were you able to let them run their natural course, consistent with the birds you were watching? What, if anything, got in the way of just watching the birds with Jesus? How can you extend this exercise to daily living, allowing your thoughts—especially the difficult thoughts you tend to fuse with surrounding an emotional disorder—to just fly on by, consistent with the birds by the

Sea of Galilee? What role can Jesus play in helping you to give over control of your thoughts to him, similar to letting go of control while observing nature?

_____

_____

_____

_____

_____

_____

Conclusion

In this chapter, you read about the defusion process, which involves seeing thoughts with more tentativeness and flexibility so you can focus on living out your values. As a Christian, watchfulness seems to parallel the defusion process, helping you to notice your thoughts with a vigilant attentiveness in order to recognize God's presence. For the early desert Christians, _nepsis_ involved noticing the inner workings of the mind, patiently reciting scripture as a way to stay focused on God. In the process, the inner terrain of the mind becomes more familiar, helping you to gently pivot towards an awareness of God's active, loving presence when your focus has been derailed.

Among the exercises in the chapter, you were able to learn about several metaphors to describe watchfulness, practicing the ability to be watchful via the Jesus Prayer. Within this practice, the goal is to cultivate sustained attention, recognizing that God is active and present in each passing moment. Whenever the mind is distracted with _logismoi_, or other forms of fused thinking surrounding emotional disorders, you can shift your attention to the Jesus Prayer in order to surrender these compulsive thoughts to him.

In the next chapter, acceptance is reviewed, which can help you relate to inner experiences with more gentleness and compassion.

Combining defusion and acceptance can allow you to relate to the inner world in a new way and focus on value-based living, rather than the inner world bullying you around, missing out on life as you struggle with distressing thoughts, feelings, and sensations. As a Christian, watchfulness (the Greek word, *nepsis*) and endurance (the Greek word, *hupomone*) can help you to follow Jesus in a new, vibrant manner, rather than allowing the *logismoi* and inner distress to sidetrack your ability to follow him as his disciple. Reminiscent of the 12 disciples' adventurous trek, your journey with Jesus can be unique and exciting, especially if you are willing to accept the pain of life. Instead of waving goodbye to Jesus as he walks away, relating to the inner world with acceptance and flexibility can help you drop your distractions and radically walk with him on the paths of life.

Notes

1 The quotes in this section are from Wortley (2012). Used with permission.
2 Often, early desert Christians viewed demons as *the* source of tempting, compulsive thoughts. My suggestion, though, is to steer clear of this more narrow interpretation. As C. S. Lewis (1942) famously stated, "There are two equal and opposite errors into which our race can fall about the devils. One is to disbelieve in their existence. *The other is to believe, and to feel an excessive and unhealthy interest in them*" (p. ix, italics added). Instead, try to focus on shifting towards relying on God's omniscience, without spending too much time seeking to understand the *exact* source of cognitive processes that get in the way of following Jesus. Nevertheless, as a more general understanding, the fall of humankind has led to prolonged, enduring difficulties with trying to be like God, especially when we rely on our own knowledge of good and evil, rather than depend on God (see Bonhoeffer, 1955, 1959).
3 See Coniaris (1998) for a summary of the Jesus Prayer, including its biblical roots.
4 This exercise is inspired by the theology of Bonhoeffer (1955, 1959), including his exegesis of the creation story in Genesis.
5 This exercise is based on Bonhoeffer's (1955) review of the Pharisees, contrasting their judgmental thinking with Jesus' focus on loving others. For Bonhoeffer, there is a clear distinction between love/simple action and knowledge of good and evil/judgment. For a more accessible review of the contrast between love and judgment in the Christian life, see Boyd (2004).
6 See Talbot (2013) for a more detailed review of the central ingredients of the Jesus Prayer.

References

Bonhoeffer, D. (1955). *Ethics.* New York: Touchstone.

Bonhoeffer, D. (1959). *Creation and Fall.* New York: Touchstone.

Boyd, G. (2004). *Repenting of Religion: Turning from Judgment to the Love Of God.* Grand Rapids, MI: Baker Books.

Burton-Christie, D. (1993). *The Word in the Desert: Scripture and the Quest for Holiness in Early Christian Monasticism.* New York: Oxford University Press.

Chryssavgis, J. (2008). *In the Heart of the Desert: The Spirituality of the Desert Fathers and Mothers.* Bloomington, IN: World Wisdom, Inc.

Coniaris, A. (1998). *Philokalia: The Bible of Orthodox Spirituality.* Minneapolis, MN: Light & Life Publishing Company.

Harmless, W. (2008). *Mystics.* New York: Oxford University Press.

Harris, R. (2009). *ACT Made Simple: An Easy-to-Read Primer on Acceptance and Commitment Therapy.* Oakland, CA: New Harbinger Publications, Inc.

Hayes, S., Strosahl, K., & Wilson, K. (2012). *Acceptance and Commitment Therapy: The Process and Practice of Mindful Change* (2nd ed.). New York: The Guilford Press.

Lane, B. (1998). *The Solace Of Fierce Landscapes: Exploring Desert and Mountain Spirituality.* New York: Oxford University Press.

Lewis, C. S. (1942). *The Screwtape Letters.* New York: HarperCollins Publishers.

Paintner, C. (2012). *Desert Fathers and Mothers: Early Christian Wisdom Sayings.* Woodstock, VT: SkyLight Paths Publishing.

Talbot, J. (2013). *The Jesus Prayer: A Cry for Mercy, a Path of Renewal.* Downers Grove, IL: InterVarsity Press.

Williams, M. (2008). *Mindfulness, depression and modes of mind. Cognitive Therapy Research, 32,* 721–733.

Wortley, J. (2012). *The Book of Elders: Sayings of the Desert Fathers.* Trappist, KY: Cistercian Publications.

Chapter 4: Acceptance and Endurance with Emotions

Introduction

In this chapter, you will learn about ACT's acceptance process, exploring a definition of acceptance—which is by no means synonymous with agreement—as well as the writings of the early desert Christians on a similar strategy. Moreover, you will learn about a way to cultivate a hopeful endurance, sitting at Jesus' feet, reminiscent of Mary in the gospel of Luke. Consistent with ACT, you will read about several metaphors that can help you to make sense of the role that acceptance plays in value-based living. In other words, acceptance is not cultivated as the end goal; rather, acceptance is used as a way to open up opportunities to pursue your values.

For Christians, this involves a hopeful, patient endurance, pressing forward because of the path that Jesus has carved out for you. Given that Jesus is the suffering servant (Isaiah 53), there will be psychological pain on the road to sanctification, or becoming more like him. Yet, as you follow Jesus, you will be living out a set of virtues in order to deepen a sense of meaning, purpose, and psychological and spiritual growth.

To conclude the chapter, you will practice several exercises in order to experientially understand acceptance, including its role in following Jesus. Along the way, you will reflect on a range of emotions you might have historically tried to avoid, which can get in the way of walking behind Christ, practice enduring painful emotions like early desert Christians, and practice two forms of contemplation, which you can carry with you into daily living. Above all else, this chapter will help you to relate differently to painful inner experiences, given that the tug-of-war with them is often more distracting than the symptoms themselves.

ACT's Acceptance Process

Within the ACT model, acceptance is intended to help you open up to your most unpleasant inner experiences, including difficult emotions linked to depressive and anxiety disorders (Hayes, Strosahl, & Wilson, 2012). With acceptance, the idea is that avoiding painful emotions has likely led to a life that does not work, given that all of your time is spent fighting pain, rather than living out your values. From an ACT perspective, pain is unavoidable in life, meaning the human condition is fraught with disappointment, loss, rejection, hurt, and the like. Stated differently, by definition, living life leads to pain.

When you experience pain, there is sort of a fork in the road (Hayes, 2005), with one path leading to acceptance and the pursuit of values. Certainly, this path leads to a town filled with the potential for distress—because the residents are willing to live out their values, they will inevitably come up short from time to time, leading to sadness, hurt, fear, and anxiety. These emotions, from this town's perspective, are by no means problematic on their own since they can also enrich daily living.

For these residents, sadness means they have missed out on something important, helping them to reconnect with their values, pursuing what matters. Anxiety is an important emotion that captures the need to take action, anticipating that something might go wrong in the future. Finally, anger helps them to understand there has been some perceived injustice that needs to be remedied, with guilt reminding them they need to make amends for a perceived slight towards another member of the community. You see, in this town, uncomfortable emotions have a purpose, and are not automatically avoided or averted. Overall, the residents fully embrace the spectrum of emotions, based on the view that the inner world offers the opportunity to experience *all* of life, rather than only the positive emotions of daily living.

The other path, though, leads to a town devoted to anesthetizing life. In this town, to be sure, there are moments of pleasure, especially when sadness, anxiety, fear, and anger are stifled. Because unpleasant emotions are not used as signals, the townspeople struggle to connect to their values, missing out on a life devoted to a deeper sense of meaning, vitality, and zeal. On any given day, many of the residents stay indoors, content with avoiding pain, utilizing a host of avoidance strategies to keep inner distress at bay. Unfortunately, though, the pain of missing out on life, wondering what the other road leads to, seems to creep regularly into daily living. Therefore, the people of this town also experience a sense of loss, wondering what it might be like to live in a community that embraces *all* of life, even its disappointments, given that taking risks can also lead to meaning and growth.

Although the above description does not fully capture the contrast between avoidance and acceptance, I believe it can serve as a useful starting point. To embrace all of life means that pain will be a part of the process. Still, from an ACT perspective, the payoff is a life devoted to the pursuit of values, rather than the elimination of pain, consistent with running a half-marathon.

In your training, you will feel pain along the way, given that your muscles are growing in preparation for the big day. When you wake up sore, you are able to make sense of this bodily experience, noting to yourself that the aches are worth it because of the task at hand. As you hear the gun go off to start the race on the big day, you experience a sense of excitement, focusing on getting to the finish line. Yet, you are also passionate about running with your fellow racers, embracing the scenery and relational connections along the way. Because you value running, so much so that you have devoted an extended period of time to train for running over a dozen miles in one outing, you embrace the pain along the way, recognizing that it is an inevitable part of the process.

This race example, consistent with the town of pain mentioned previously, can serve as a fitting example of the inevitability of pain when something matters to you greatly. To run the race, you are by no means only focused on experiencing pleasure. In fact, the task at hand involves a much more complicated picture. Because of the sacrifice you are making, you are able to make room for pain, accepting that it is a part of the journey, reminiscent of life in general.

For ACT practitioners, there are a plethora of phrases that are used to describe the process of acceptance (adapted from Harris, 2009):

- Leaning into the experience
- Opening up to the experience
- Making room for the experience
- Making peace with the experience
- Expanding around the experience

As noted in the above descriptions, rephrasing inner pain can help you to relate to it with a bit more openness, flexibility, tentativeness, and non-judgment, rather than fusing with what your mind says about your inner pain. When you are able to experience inner pain directly, rather than letting your mind jump in to interpret your pain with labels, judgments, and evaluations, it can be easier to make room for it in order to pivot towards value-based living.

To offer one more example, imagine you are singing passionately in your church, fully connected to the experience of worshipping God on a Sunday morning. On this beautiful day, there just so happens to be someone sitting next to you who does not have a good singing voice. As you are belting out the worship music, inspired by the Psalms, you are repeatedly distracted by this unpleasant voice.

Rather quickly, your mind begins to jump in, stating that the person is inconsiderate: "Doesn't he know he is ruining it for everyone else?" As your mind offers evaluations of what is happening, you notice that your frustration continues to grow. A light bulb goes off, and you recognize that this person—a child of God, like you— is attempting to glorify God through his own attempts at worship, which is just as vital to his spiritual growth as your worship is to your spiritual trajectory. As you realize this, you thank your mind for chiming in, before returning to your experience. Now, as you listen to him, you can experience his voice directly, without your mind getting in the way.

As you begin to experience your emotions directly, rather than to fuse with rules, evaluations, judgments, and clever reasons for avoidance (Harris, 2009), you may find that you can expand around your emotional experiences, recognizing that you have much more space for them. In other words, as you let go of your judgments, your emotions can run their natural course—they might even be helpful in enriching your life, given that sadness, fear, anxiety, guilt, and anger are vital in navigating the most difficult terrains of life, offering a sort of thrust for value-based living. Interestingly, early desert Christians similarly described relating to inner experiences with more patience and tentativeness, even adding a sense of hope, referred to as *hupomone*.

Early Desert Christians and Endurance
Among the early desert Christians, an important part of daily living involved "staying put" in their cell. Rather than constantly moving from place to place, the monks who resided in the deserts of Egypt, Syria, and Palestine would make it a point to stay in one place. From both a psychological and spiritual perspective, the purpose of staying in the cell involved getting to know what was going on within the

inner world, cultivating the ability to focus on God's active, loving present as each moment unfolded.[1]

Deepening their ability to endure, with an attitude of hope and patience, was key. Thus, a hopeful endurance (the Greek word, *hupomone*) captures the ability to stay present to whatever experiences arise, faithfully attending to what is happening because God is present (Chryssavgis, 2008; Paintner, 2012). This term, used over two-dozen times in the New Testament, describes a plant that continues to grow, despite being rooted in a harsh environment (Barclay, 2000). Therefore, to be hopeful, enduring the difficult inner world of depressive or anxiety-related symptoms, means to continue to push forward. For Christian monks within the desert, they experienced an added sense of hope because God resided with them in the cell, helping them as they faced a variety of unpleasant inner events from day to day.

The following teachings from the *Sayings of the Desert Fathers*[2] seem to capture endurance within the cell, offering an accurate view of the importance of patience in monastic life:

- "The mark of the monk becomes apparent in temptations."
- "Eat, drink, and sleep, only do not leave your cell, knowing that remaining patiently in the cell brings a monk up to what he should be."
- "Go, stay in your cell; give your body as a warranty to the wall of your cell, and do not come out of there. Let your [thoughts] think what [they like], but do not put your body out of your cell."
- "Just as an opponent fights in wrestling matches, so ought the wrestler (meaning the monk) to withstand his [thoughts], stretching out his hands to heaven and calling on God for aid."

As the above sayings reveal, the purpose of enduring in the cell was to face the various temptations that arose from day to day, staying present to inner experiences. The reason why difficult inner events can be endured, certainly, is because God is with you, helping you through a variety of intrapsychic challenges as each moment unfolds.

Endurance in the Bible
Interestingly, the Bible mentions this type of a hopeful, patient endurance (the Greek word, *hupomone*) several times in the New Testament. As one example, in the first chapter of 2 Corinthians, the Apostle Paul mentioned that God comforts Christians who are "in

any trouble," acknowledging that Jesus' sufferings are shared among the Body of Christ. In fact, Paul went on to state the following in 2 Corinthians 1:5–7:

- "For just as we share abundantly in the sufferings of Christ, so also our comfort abounds through Christ. If we are distressed, it is for your comfort and salvation; if we are comforted, it is for your comfort, which produces in you *patient endurance* [italics added] of the same sufferings we suffer. And our hope for you is firm, because we know that just as you share in our sufferings, so also you share in our comfort."

Here, you will see that Paul is acknowledging the significant challenges inevitable in the Christian life; yet, suffering is not experienced in isolation. Rather, Christians suffer with Jesus, receiving comfort along the way.

As another example, *hupomone* is used seven times in Revelation, capturing the hope and endurance that is necessary in Christian living, given the 1st-century church's ongoing struggles. When used in this context, persecuted Christians had hope in Jesus' eventual return, pressing forward in spite of the pain they were facing. Stated differently, despite the life and death crises many were experiencing, they were able to accept their painful conditions because of the firm trust they placed in Jesus.

In a 21st-century context, you may be experiencing tremendous pain, facing the symptoms of an emotional disorder on a daily basis. However, because of the hope you have in Jesus, including God's eventual restoration of this fallen world, you can confidently march forward, walking faithfully behind your Lord and Savior as you carry out his will for your life. Thus, a hopeful endurance in contemporary society means focusing on the task at hand—walking with Jesus along a well worn, beaten path, ready to go where he wants you to go.

Endurance and the Mary Mode

In Luke's gospel, Mary simply sat at the feet of Jesus, focusing on him as Martha scurried about, anxiously driven to "fix" her environment. For Mary, the present moment was about yielding to Jesus' presence, patiently listening to him. For Christians struggling with emotional disorders, this Mary state of mind can be especially helpful, given the emphasis on simply sitting at Jesus' feet, with nowhere else to be and nothing else to do, yielding to his providential care.

To add another layer of understanding to the Mary mode, cultivating a hopeful, patient endurance while sitting at Jesus' feet can be particularly important since there is a point of focus and emphasis on Jesus' eventual return. In other words, being able to endure inner pain is possible because Christians can focus their attention on Jesus, who modeled the ability to persevere in the face of tremendous pain. For Christians throughout the ages, a hopeful endurance is possible because of the faith placed in Jesus—he is the reason endurance is possible, given that he suffered, too, and carved out a path for Christians to follow him on.

As a second point, while sitting at Jesus' feet, like Mary, endurance is possible because God will eventually restore all things, meaning that the pain in this life is not a permanent reality. Acknowledging the inevitability of pain in this fallen world is important in order to understand the task at hand—following Jesus in spite of inner distress. Because psychological pain is temporary, Christians can place a firm hope in a different reality, making endurance at this moment possible. This dynamic is reminiscent of a long distance runner seeing the finish line in sight, motivating him or her to continue the race.

To draw a parallel with your life, you may be currently struggling with a long list of symptoms associated with an emotional disorder; yet, recognizing that Jesus will eventually return, you can work towards patiently sitting at his feet, focusing exclusively on him and acknowledging that his presence is enough for now. In other words, rather than frantically hurrying about, anxiously driven to "fix," like Martha, you can approach your situation as Mary might, capturing the ability to sit patiently in one place, given that Jesus' presence is sufficient. Perseverance is also possible based on the eschatological reality of Jesus' eventual return.

Endurance Metaphors

In addition to thinking about acceptance and a hopeful, patient endurance in the context of the story of Mary and Martha in Luke, it may be helpful to consider a few other biblical metaphors to make sense of acceptance:

- Acceptance/hopeful endurance is like Paul's thorn mentioned in 2 Corinthians 12; since he was able to reinterpret his "thorn" as a blessing from God, allowing him to humbly trust in God to sustain him, maybe I can see God's providence in my depressive or anxiety-related symptoms, making room for them as I follow Jesus.

- Acceptance/hopeful endurance is like committing to going home, reminiscent of the Parable of the Lost Son in Luke 15; in spite of the pain I am feeling, I can run into God's loving arms, trusting that he will embrace me and celebrate with me, eager for my return.
- Acceptance/hopeful endurance is like embracing the anxiety Noah and his family might have faced in the Old Testament, uncertain about what was next as they waited patiently on the ark for the waters to recede; yet, they continued to press forward, confident that God had a plan for them, in spite of their likely uncertainty.
- Acceptance/hopeful endurance is like the Apostle Paul being imprisoned (see Philippians 1), confident that being jailed would somehow advance the gospel message. In my own life, I can accept the inner experiences and life circumstances that I cannot change, looking for God's sovereignty and infinite wisdom in the process.
- Acceptance/hopeful endurance is like Jesus in the Garden of Gethsemane in the Gospels, accepting 'the cup' that his Father offered, pressing forward to the cross in spite of his agony and anxiety about what was yet to come. In my own life, I can work towards surrendering to God's will, making room for painful experiences, reminiscent of Jesus.

In these biblical examples, the characters were faced with difficult circumstances, which likely led to significant psychological pain, an inevitable part of life. Still, because of their faith in God, they were able to press forward, accepting the pain based on the firm hope they placed in God's sovereign, loving hand guiding the outcome.

Exercise: Listing Distressing Emotions You Have Tried to Avoid
At this point in the chapter, it may be helpful to move from a more abstract understanding of acceptance/hopeful endurance to a concrete picture in your current life. If possible, try to list the painful emotions you have historically tried to avoid. In particular, you might have attempted to avoid anxiety, sadness, anger, fear, or shame, consistent with a range of biblical characters' emotional experiences in the Bible.

Try to reflect on the actual emotional experience, sinking into what it might have felt like as you utilized an avoidance strategy to attempt to make the pain go away. Then, try to document the cost of avoidance, in terms of how the avoidance strategy might have led to you missing out on life. Finally, try to document how the outcome might have been different, should you have continued, enduring the pain and living out your relationship with God.

Emotion I Tried to Avoid	Cost of Avoidance (Negative Outcome)	Positive Outcome if I Would Have Endured the Emotion
In the last six months or so, I have tried to avoid anxiety by not going to church.	Because I stopped going to church, I missed out on building relationships within my church community.	If I had continued to go to church, in spite of the anxiety, I might have built some key relationships to help me in my current situation at work.

As you reflect on the exercise, really try to consider how life might have been different if you would have accepted the inevitability of the emotion, almost like accepting that you live with an imperfect roommate, who is sometimes sloppy, inconsiderate, and rude. Because the lease is not up for another year, you have to find a way to make peace with him, or otherwise suffer because of ruminative and worrying thoughts about being stuck, wishing he would just go away.

In the Christian life, if possible, try to contrast using avoidance versus acceptance, focusing on the outcome of following Jesus—which strategy, avoidance or acceptance, can help you to carry out God's will in the long run? Which strategy, if any, tends to keep you stuck?

Exercise: Enduring Emotions in the "Cell"
For this exercise, I would like you to consider what it might have been like for early desert Christians some 1,700 years ago in the deserts of Egypt and Syria. Given the heat, dry landscape, and inactivity in the

desert, what might it have been like to face both the inner world and God, who they had to depend utterly on because they lived in such a harsh environment? More specifically, try to imagine the dedication that it must have taken to take up residence in a small room, devoting each day to prayer, scripture reading, and basic tasks (e.g., basket weaving).

In your cell, as an early desert Christian, you longed to connect with God, relying on him for a sense of safety, comfort, and connection. Because you spent most of your time there, you had to face the reality that there was nowhere else to turn to find him. Within the walls of the cell was the only place, whether you liked it or not, that you would meet God on a daily basis.

Within the silence and stillness of the cell, your inner world was a significant source of distraction, given that you had to face your memories, evaluations, judgments, temptations, painful emotions, and uncomfortable sensations, such as physiological pain and hunger. In the confines of the cell, of course, you inevitably had to find a way to endure, with the hope that God would help you, given he is infinitely wise, good, and powerful.

Certainly, there was the opportunity to experience tremendous joy in the cell, too, even when facing the *logismoi* (i.e., tempting thoughts) that seemed to attack your sustained attention on God. Therefore, to trust in God, you began to focus on his word, especially the Psalms, returning over and over again to his promises in the Bible. Eventually, you repeated short phrases in order to be especially attentive to his presence, resting in him in the present moment, even when facing unpleasant thoughts, feelings, and sensations. Over time, you were able to deepen your awareness of his presence, getting to know the workings of your inner life.

Fast-forward to the 21st century, and try to reflect on the below questions, especially in the context of enduring inner experiences within the walls of the cell:

- What is the location, if any, of my "cell" in the 21st century? Where do I go to be with God in solitude?
- In this location, how can I practice endurance, stripping away the sounds and distractions of the world and completely rely on God in silence?
- In other words, how can I begin to view the ability to endure as a positive aspect of spiritual and psychological growth, helping me

to deepen my relationship with God, rather than an obstacle to pleasure and "happiness" in my life?

- What role, if any, will this patient attentiveness play in daily living? Can resting with God in silence, enduring painful inner experiences, somehow prepare me for my walk with Jesus each and every day? If so, how?
- What psychological insights can the desert monks from roughly 1,700 years ago teach me about enduring pain in order to be present to God's loving attentiveness, surrendering to his providence from moment to moment? Why might they have chosen to stay in their cell for so long? How did residing in their cell help them respond to psychological struggles more effectively, as well as deepen their relationship with God over time?

Exercise: Be Still

I would like you first to read Psalm 46, noted below, reflecting on your ability to let go of your avoidance efforts in order to be still in the presence of God, who is sovereign. More to the point, Psalm 46:10 uses the Hebrew word, *raphah*, meaning to "cease striving," with the New International Version of the Bible translating the term as "be still" (Strong, 2001). Used just after the psalmist's claim that God destroys weapons on the battlefield, some have interpreted the "be still" phrase to mean something along the lines of "set down your weapons" (Earwood, 1989).

- "God is our refuge and strength, an ever-present help in trouble. Therefore, we will not fear, though the earth give way, and the mountains fall into the heart of the sea, though its waters roar and foam and the mountains quake with their surging. There is a river whose streams make glad the city of God, the holy place where the Most High dwells. God is within her; she will not fall; God will help her at break of day. Nations are in uproar, kingdoms fall; he lifts his voice, the earth melts. The Lord Almighty is with us; the God of Jacob is our fortress. Come and see what the Lord has done, the desolations he has brought on the earth. He makes wars cease to the ends of the earth. He breaks the bow and shatters the spear; he burns the shields with fire. He says, *'Be still, and know that I am God* [italics added]; I will be exalted among the nations, I will be exalted in the earth.' The Lord Almighty is with us; the God of Jacob is our fortress."

In this exercise, I would like for you to imagine that you are on a battlefield, using every weapon imaginable to avoid your pain. Whatever weapons you have used in the past, your job is to simply lay them down, right now, given that God is in control. In other words, God can destroy every weapon, including your best avoidance strategies. Because God is sovereign, you can stop all of your attempts to avoid your pain.

When you are ready, close your eyes and begin to repeat the phrase, "be still." You may want to inhale, "be," and exhale, "still." Try this activity for about ten minutes, with each in-breath capturing your willingness to let go of all of your own efforts at striving towards symptom elimination. Instead, just rest in God's presence, recognizing that he is God. Continue for about ten minutes total, sinking into the phrase, "be still." If you can, try not to move in any way, feeling God's presence as he surrounds you with his loving arms. There is nowhere else to be and nothing else to do as you drop all of your weapons on the battlefield, ceasing all needless activity because God will protect you.

Now, see if you can reflect on this exercise, writing down some of your reactions to the "be still" meditation.

_____

_____

_____

_____

_____

_____

_____

_____

Exercise: Centering Prayer with a Prayer Word
Within the contemplative Christian tradition, early desert Christians recited scripture in order to focus their attention on God, often repeating the Psalms as a way to cultivate a deeper sense of God's

active presence.[3] Eventually, longer phrases were condensed into a few words, which evolved into a wordless form of prayer, referred to as *apophatic prayer*.[4] In this form of prayer, which is contrasted with *cataphatic prayer*, wherein Christians use words to converse with God, the purpose is to let go of the tendency to use words, phrases, and thinking itself to relate to God. In other words, contemplatives throughout the ages have sought to rest in God's presence, sitting in silence. Whenever their attention drifts to a thought, feeling, or sensation, monks have historically used a prayer word to refocus on God's presence.

In the 21st century, *centering prayer* (Keating, 2006) is used to help Christians recognize that God is active and present, employing a prayer word as a way to symbolically surrender to God, who is "working behind the scenes," so to speak. Within centering prayer, Christians take the following three steps (adapted from Frenette, 2012):

- To begin, select a word (usually with a single syllable, such as "God" or "love") to capture your willingness to yield to God's active, loving presence.
- Get into a comfortable position, close your eyes, and begin to gently repeat the word silently to yourself, which reflects a submissive, surrendering posture towards God.
- Eventually, you will become distracted with a thought, feeling, or sensation; when you have been pulled away from the prayer word, slowly return to the repetition of the word, with an attitude of non-judgment and compassion.
- When the time comes to a close, try to sit silently for a few minutes, resting in God's loving arms.

With centering prayer, the purpose is to surrender to God's providence, sitting in silence with him, reminiscent of Mary sitting at the feet of Jesus in the Gospel of Luke. Within this type of contemplative practice, the purpose is to be focused on God in the present moment, cultivating an attitude of compassion and non-judgment towards the inner world. Given that thoughts, feelings, and sensations are neither pursued nor pushed away, you may find that you are able to relate to the inner world with more gentleness and tentativeness during this wordless, imageless time with God.

From my perspective, there are at least two benefits of centering prayer when applying the practice to emotional disorders. To begin, you are working on your ability to rest in God's presence, letting go of the need to "fix," problem solve, and the like. Instead, the focus is on yielding to God's loving, infinite wisdom, deepening your trust in his ability to "work behind the scenes."

It is almost as if you live in a home with a basement, calling a plumber to check the pipes beneath the first floor of your home. When the plumber rings the doorbell, you invite him in, receiving him into your home. In turn, he walks down the stairs to the basement. Since you are sitting on the first floor, you do not know what he is doing exactly, yet you are aware that he is actively working beneath you. Therefore, you trust that he is doing what he is supposed to be doing. Because it is his job to work on the pipes, you can let go of your own efforts to inspect and fix the pipes. This ability to let go of your own striving, of course, means that you can simply rest when he is downstairs.

Beyond resting in God's presence during centering prayer, the practice can help you relate to your inner world with more open curiosity, deepening your ability to allow your thoughts, feelings, and sensations to do what they will do, without trying to chase them or push them away. Given that you are focused on your prayer word (e.g., "God," "love," "Abba"), you can simply acknowledge the inner experience that has pulled you away from symbolically gazing upon God, before slowly and gently returning to your loving attentiveness, reminiscent of Mary sitting at the feet of Jesus.

Overall, applied to emotional disorders, centering prayer can help you let go of the tendency to want to rid yourself of unpleasant inner experiences, which often exacerbates your symptoms, especially when they will not go away. By accepting the inner world, you are working on deepening your ability to endure psychological pain with an attitude of trust and hope, patiently waiting upon God to work within. Of course, the purpose of centering prayer is not to eventually get rid of your pain; rather, the daily practice can help you surrender to God, resting in his loving arms and connecting to an awareness of his presence from moment to moment throughout your day.

What follows is a sample transcript of centering prayer. My hope is that you are eventually able to utilize centering prayer on your own, rather than relying on the below guide.

- When you are ready, get into a comfortable position, closing your eyes and sitting up straight in a quiet environment. First, pray to God that he will be active and present during this 20-minute period, sitting in silence with him. Maybe ask that he help you to surrender to him, giving up all efforts to change, fix, or avoid the inner world. Once you have said a brief prayer to God, begin to recite the word "surrender," using the word to represent your willingness to yield to his providential care. There is nowhere else to be and absolutely nothing else to do as you sit in silence with him. As you repeat the word, practice letting go of all efforts to change your inner world, trusting that he is in charge of your inner life. In other words, you are relinquishing control to him, allowing your inner world to do what it will do, without jumping in to alter it in any way.

Over and over again, gently recite the word, "surrender," letting it marinate, representing your willingness to let go. When you notice that your mind has wandered to a thought, feeling, or sensation (which will likely happen sooner rather than later), just acknowledge that you have shifted your focus. Non-judgmentally and compassionately return to your prayer word. If this happens every few seconds, it is perfectly okay. The mind can be quite restless. Therefore, offer yourself grace and mercy as you continue to shift your focus back to your prayer word—"surrender."

Remember that repeating your prayer word symbolizes your yielding posture, reminiscent of Mary sitting at the feet of Jesus. Each time you say the word, "surrender," you are asking God to be active and present within the inner world; therefore, there is nothing you need to do on your end. Trusting in him and letting go of your own efforts are all you are "doing."

Continue to acknowledge your thoughts, feelings, and sensations when you notice your attention has been pulled away from your prayer word until the practice comes to a close. When you are done, just sit in silence for a minute or two, resting in God's presence. If possible, try to take this practice with you as you move about your day, connecting to his active, loving presence from moment to moment.

When you are done, try to write down a few reactions to the practice, including what it was like to work on letting go of your own efforts, resting in God's presence.

_____

_____

_____

_____

_____

_____

_____

_____

_____

_____

Exercise: The Welcoming Prayer

Related to centering prayer, the _welcoming prayer_ (Bourgeault, 2004) is a contemplative strategy designed to help you continue to deepen your relationship with God throughout your day. Consisting of three steps, the purpose is to welcome unpleasant emotions, inviting God into the experience (adapted from Bourgeault, 2004):

- Pay attention to where the emotion is being experienced in the body, "sinking into" the emotion.
- Welcome the emotional experience, rather than trying to push it away, inviting God to be present with you as you fully embrace the inner pain.
- Relinquish all efforts to change the emotion, letting it slowly drift away into the background without trying to push it away.

Reminiscent of early desert Christians' willingness to endure painful emotions in the cell, cultivating an attitude of hope and patience, this practice can help you learn to lean into emotional pain, given that God is with you. Although the practice may seem counterintuitive, striving to remain with the pain can help you relate differently to it, ameliorating the distress you are in. Although the emotional pain might not go away, you are inviting God to be with you within the inner world, the "cell," so that you can persevere with confidence and encouragement, following Jesus while in pain.

This exercise overlaps significantly with exposure therapy within the psychotherapy literature. For a variety of emotional disorders, avoiding pain can get in the way of living life. Therefore, with exposure therapy, clients learn to face inner distress, which can allow them to live life again, recognizing that the pain they are in does not have to get in the way of meaningful, vibrant living. Overall, deepening your ability to accept inner pain, enduring with a sense of hope and confidence because Jesus is with you, can help you to walk with him wherever he would like for you to go.

In the space that follows, see if you can set at least three goals for using the welcoming prayer in daily life. For example, you might commit to using the welcoming prayer during three salient moments throughout your day, welcoming sadness or anxiety during key instances in your life. During your lunch break, possibly, you can set a goal of welcoming anxiety about social situations, asking God to be with you as you endure the inner experience and let go of the tendency to attempt to avoid the emotion.

1 _____

_____

2 _____

_____

3 _____

_____

Exercise: Sitting at the Feet of Jesus

As the final exercise for the chapter, building on (a) prior exercises, (b) the story of Mary and Martha in the gospel of Luke, and (c) the "being" mode of the mind (Williams, 2008), I would like for you to get into a comfortable position, closing your eyes and sitting up straight, alert to God's active presence.

When you are ready, I would like for you to imagine that you are actually in Mary and Martha's home with Jesus, literally sitting at his feet. Within this room, many people are talking and eating together, which is somewhat distracting. Also, Martha seems to be anxiously preparing the meal in the background, visibly upset. As you notice these distractions, try to stay focused on Jesus' presence, imagining that you are attentively looking at him, especially when the background noise grows.

Each time you notice that an emotion arises within your inner world in response to the background noise, just acknowledge the experience, before gently returning to your gaze. If you experience the emotion of frustration, given that other people seem to be loud and rude, just notice the emotion, turning your head ever so slightly back to Jesus. If you experience anxiety, with Martha sort of rubbing off on you, just note that the anxiety is present, and pivot back to Jesus' position in the room. If you experience sadness, with your mind being pulled away to a recent loss (or the anticipation that Jesus will be leaving soon), just sink into the experience for a few seconds, before attentively refocusing on Jesus.

In sum, the purpose of this exercise is to practice gazing upon God, cultivating an attitude of acceptance as you focus your attention on him. Rather than fighting against all the distractions in the room (which symbolize daily living), just note when your mind has drifted, before gently and non-judgmentally returning to listening to Jesus. In the space that follows, see if you can reflect on the experience, exploring what it was like to practice non-judgment, especially when powerful emotions arose within the inner world.

_____

_____

_____

_____

_____

_____

_____

_____

Conclusion

In this chapter, you explored the ACT process of acceptance, learning about the importance of letting go of the tendency to fight with (or avoid) unpleasant inner experiences, given that focusing on symptom elimination can get in the way of following Jesus. Along the way, you learned about the early desert Christians' experience of staying in the cell, despite some of the unpleasant inner experiences that likely arose from minute to minute. Also, you were able to unpack some key metaphors that can help you to cultivate an attitude of acceptance, enduring with a sense of hope and patience because of Jesus' example and eventual return.

In terms of some of the exercises, my hope is that you were able to "try on" acceptance, deepening your ability to endure because Jesus is with you in each passing moment. Since you are walking with him, it may be easier to make room for inner pain, given that you are not alone. What is more, because you are yielding to his providence, building trust along the way, you can let go of your own tendencies to judge your unpleasant emotions, recognizing that he has a plan for you in this life and the next.

In the next chapter, you will be exploring the present-moment awareness process in ACT, learning about the overlap between the ability to connect with each passing moment and the desert monks' emphasis on silence and stillness with God. When rooted in the present, emotional disorders can lose their hold on you, given that they often involve ruminating about the past or worrying about the future. In addition, God is located in the present moment; as a disciple of Jesus, therefore, staying focused on him from day to day and minute to minute can help you to live an exciting, vibrant life, filled with adventure and hope as you trek with him down the roads he has chosen for you to follow him on.

Notes

1 See Chryssavgis (2008) and Paintner (2012) for more detailed summaries of monks' relationship with the "cell."
2 The quotes in this section are from Wortley (2012). Used with permission.
3 For a review of the evolution of the "prayer word" in contemplative practice, see Laird (2006).
4 For a discussion on *apophatic* and *cataphatic* forms of prayer, see Bourgeault (2004).

References

Barclay, W. (2000). *New Testament Words.* Louisville, KY: Westminster John Knox Press.

Bourgeault, C. (2004). *Centering Prayer and Inner Awakening.* Lanham, MD: Cowley Publications.

Chryssavgis, J. (2008). *In the Heart of the Desert: The Spirituality of the Desert Fathers and Mothers.* Bloomington, IN: World Wisdom, Inc.

Earwood, G. (1989). Psalm 46. *Review and Expositor, 86,* 79–86.

Frenette, D. (2012). *The Path of Centering Prayer: Deepening Your Experience of God.* Boulder, CO: Sounds True, Inc.

Harris, R. (2009). *ACT Made Simple: An Easy-to-Read Primer on Acceptance and Commitment Therapy.* Oakland, CA: New Harbinger Publications, Inc.

Hayes, S. (2005). *Get Out of Your Mind and Into Your Life: The New Acceptance & Commitment Therapy.* Oakland, CA: New Harbinger Publications, Inc.

Hayes, S., Strosahl, K., & Wilson, K. (2012). *Acceptance and Commitment Therapy: The Process and Practice of Mindful Change* (2nd ed.). New York: The Guilford Press.

Keating, T. (2006). *Open Mind, Open Heart, 20th Anniversary Edition.* New York: Continuum.

Laird, M. (2006). *Into the Silent Land: A Guide to the Christian Practice of Contemplation.* New York: Oxford University Press.

Paintner, C. (2012). *Desert Fathers and Mothers: Early Christian Wisdom Sayings.* Woodstock, VT: SkyLight Paths Publishing.

Strong, J. (2001). *The New Strong's Expanded Dictionary of the Words in the Hebrew Bible.* Nashville, TN: Thomas Nelson.

Williams, M. (2008). Mindfulness, depression and modes of mind. *Cognitive Therapy Research, 32,* 721–733.

Wortley, J. (2012). *The Book of Elders: Sayings of the Desert Fathers.* Trappist, KY: Cistercian Publications.

Chapter 5: Present-Moment Awareness and Stillness and Silence with God

Introduction

In this chapter, you will explore ACT's present-moment awareness process, learning more about the importance of the here and now in daily life. In particular, you will unpack the relationship between the past and future and emotional disorders, as well as develop an awareness of God's active, loving presence through several exercises. Building on prior chapters, you will learn about the salience of silence and stillness in early desert writings, spending time with God as you surrender to him.

Overall, present-moment awareness is an essential component of the ACT model, given that value-based action occurs with each step you take, pressing forward in the here and now. Differently stated, life is fully lived—guided by values—in the present moment, rather than at some other point in time. As a Christian, Jesus is inviting you to follow him at this moment, instead of at some other point in time in a distant future that might never come to fruition.

ACT's Present-Moment Awareness Process

Within the ACT model, *present-moment awareness* involves being rooted in the here and now, rather than lost in the mind, preoccupied with the past or future (Hayes, Strosahl, & Wilson, 2012). In other words, with this important process, you are able to focus your attention in a way that you are not distracted by the inner world, pulled away from each unfolding second, one after another. Often, you may be distracted by the past, including stories about prior events or memories that get in the way of values in the present moment. As another struggle, you may be preoccupied with the future, worrying about some sort of disaster that seems to be just around the corner.

From an ACT perspective, now is the only time that exists. On the other hand, the past and future are accessed through the world of language, with carefully crafted stories about who you "know" yourself to be, or yet to be determined outcomes reliant upon your own written narrative of your life. From this angle, you may be especially distracted by verbal descriptions, overly relying on them at the expense of the new life that is calling out to you in the present moment.

It is almost as if you have a friend sitting in front of you, talking to you in the present moment. You are thinking about *prior* conversations with him, distracted by ruminative thoughts about what you might have said to him last week. Or, you might be anticipating what your friend will say in 20 minutes, worrying that the conversation will turn sour. To be present in the here and now requires that you focus on the interpersonal exchange with your friend that is unfolding directly in front of you, rather than overriding this direct encounter by choosing to draw from words or images in your mind.

In ACT, *mindfulness* is often employed to make sense of present-moment awareness (Harris, 2009). Essentially, mindfulness is about focusing on one thing at a time in the present moment, letting your thoughts and feelings run their natural course, without attempting to hold onto them or push them away. As you break these ingredients down into smaller parts, notice there is a focus, a time, and a distinct relationship with thoughts and feelings:

- With mindfulness, attention is usually devoted to one thing at a time, rather than letting the mind wander from one point of focus to another.
- With mindfulness, attention is devoted to the here and now, rather than reflecting on the past or anticipating the future.
- With mindfulness, thoughts and feelings are gently acknowledged with an attitude of non-judgment and compassion (no matter what the thoughts or feelings might be), before returning to the pre-established point of focus.

Based on this very general definition, it is easy to see how mindfulness can be applied to a whole host of activities, focusing on either the inner or outer world. When turning to the inner world, the breath is often used, given that breathing is an anchor to the present moment. Or, the five senses can be employed, mindfully tasting a meal, watching the waves on the beach, listening to a record, feeling the temperature of the water while washing dishes, or smelling the aroma of fresh baked cookies coming out of the oven. Of course, the main point is that your focus is on one thing at a time in the here and now, allowing your thoughts and feelings to run their natural course without clutching them or trying to get rid of them.

To draw a parallel with nature, when you are watching a sunset, you are not trying to control the sun in any way, given you recognize your task is simply to watch what is unfolding in front of you. Moreover, you are probably not going to judge the sunset as "wrong" by any means. Finally, given that the sunset is taking place in the present moment, right in front of you, you are keenly aware that your primary task is to simply watch this particular sunset on this specific day in this unique minute of this distinct hour, allowing the Earth to rotate on its own.

Another way of describing mindfulness is that you are having a direct experience of something, rather than relying on your mind's interpretation of the encounter. With this intentional relationship, your mind can quickly jump in to judge, evaluate, and criticize the experience, which can pull you out of your connection to what is in front of you. Based on this understanding, mindfulness skills can help you to deepen your ability to practice non-judgment and compassion from moment to moment.

To apply mindfulness to emotional disorders, you may be currently struggling with depression or anxiety, ruminating about the past or worrying about the future. In fact, quite often, emotional disorders involve a past or future focus, rather than staying rooted in the present moment. With major depressive disorder, for example, you may be ruminating about the past, experiencing significant guilt based on a conversation or event you keep playing in your head over and over again. As another example, you may be anticipating a hopeless future, filling in the blanks of a yet to be determined life ahead of you, predicting that nothing will work out right.

With anxiety disorders, including panic disorder, social anxiety disorder, and generalized anxiety disorder, you might be anticipating that something will go wrong in the days, weeks, months, or years ahead, fully convinced that doom and catastrophe await you. When your mind convinces you that life will eventually be unbearable or unmanageable, your anxiety increases. As you experience more anxiety, firmly committed to believing your mind's prediction, you may avoid life, given your mind has provided "factual" information.

In each of these instances, your mind can quickly escort you to the past or future, rather than focusing on what is in front of you. It is sort of like the mind is your tour guide, with a time machine (Harris, 2009), taking you to experiences from your past and beaming you into the future. When this happens, your attention is impaired in the here and now, given that the tour is taking place in your mind, which requires quite a bit of mental energy.

Yet, with mindfulness, the purpose is to help you to rely less on this tour guide, who seems to have the best intentions (but is distracting you from enjoying the "sunsets" of life), and more on a direct experience of the here and now. It is almost as if you are saying to the tour guide, "Thanks for the offer, but I'm going to check out this mountain on my own, with a sense of excitement, newness, and curiosity, rather than relying on your commentary."

In fact, from an ACT perspective, being planted in the here and now can help you focus on living out your values, rather than paying for the tour guide, who will often give you his or her own interpretation of the scenery. When you are able to let your thoughts and feelings run their natural course, without overly relying on them to interpret each unfolding moment, you may find that you have new opportunities in life, given that you are more aware of what is in front of you. Instead of following the tour guide on the roads of life, you can head in the direction that matters to you most. After all, it is your vacation.

To offer a biblical example of present-moment awareness, if possible, try to imagine what it might have been like to be one of Jesus' disciples in the 1st century. Following Jesus on a daily basis, you would have likely been fully committed to him, absorbing his teachings and learning from watching him interact with others. Hopefully, if you were in his inner circle, you would be especially aware of his presence. You would notice his facial expressions, tone of voice, personality characteristics, and a range of other qualities that made him both fully human and fully God.

As you walked with him, ate with him, and, above all else, shared life with him, there was a sense that there was nowhere else to be and nothing else to do. In fact, believing in his message of hope, redemption, and restoration—the "good news" about what he was born to do—this was the most important time in history to be alive. Because of this awareness, you would have been especially present, alert, and aware, soaking up the time, basking in each unfolding moment spent with your Lord.

On the other hand, try to imagine what it might have been like if you were preoccupied and distracted, struggling to stay focused on your relationship with him. At times, you may have been lost within your own thoughts, worrying about getting back home or ruminating about an argument you had several years prior with a family member. In this state of distraction, you may have found that you were frequently trying to catch up to Jesus, wandering away from the group and forgetting about the key role you played among the chosen few, tasked with directly learning from him before he departed.

To bring this scenario into the present day, which type of a disciple do you identify with in your daily life—the fully present disciple or the distracted, forgetful, wandering disciple? Which type of a disciple do you wish to be, if given the chance to walk faithfully behind Jesus? To ask a more pressing question, can you passionately follow Jesus, as your Lord, if you are rooted in the past or future, ruminating about prior experiences or anticipating future catastrophes? After all, he is right in front of you—there is no better time to be alive.

In addition to ACT's perspective—present-moment awareness is crucial for value-based living, leaning into and embracing both the inner and outer world—early desert Christians had a lot to say on the topic. After all, God is active and present in each unfolding moment, given he is a personal, relational God who lovingly pursues his creation. Therefore, what follows is a review of early desert Christians' views on the present moment, including their pursuit of a calm, silent, attentive state of mind by focusing exclusively on God.

Early Desert Christians and Stillness and Silence with God
Within the *Sayings of the Desert Fathers*, stillness and silence (i.e., *hesychia*) with God is a foundational concept that permeates their various teachings. This desire for inner silence, a sort of intrinsic quietness, was especially salient for desert monks. For these desert dwellers, *hesychia* was a way to prevent the inner world from getting in the way of virtuous action in the Christian life (Harmless, 2004). What is more, stillness was about cultivating an awareness of God's presence while in their cell. Stated differently, stillness among the early desert Christians was about an awareness of the inner world, pivoting towards surrendering to God in the process (Chryssavgis, 2008).

As noted in prior chapters, monks would frequently struggle with the inner world as time passed within the walls of the cell. As a result, stillness was a way to focus their attention on God and resist the temptation to be pulled into the world of distracting, compulsive thoughts, which might also take the form of memories or emotions. In fact, a sort of "peace of mind" emerged from the confines of the cell, cultivating a quiet, restful inner world because of their ability to get to know what was happening inside, watching with a vigilant attentiveness (Harmless, 2004).

Certainly, even the word "monk" can be interpreted as "simple," with the early desert Christians focusing single-mindedly on letting go of all distractions to devote themselves entirely to God (Stewart, 2015). Therefore, paralleling ACT's present-moment awareness, early desert spirituality emphasized a point of attention (i.e., God) in the here and now (i.e., where God interacts with humankind), relating to tempting, compulsive thoughts (i.e., the *logismoi*) with a watchful vigilance in order to avoid being distracted. Rather than cultivating sustained attention by focusing solely on the breath or one of the senses, early desert Christians recited the Psalms and other passages in scripture to stay rooted in God's promises (see Wortley, 2012).

To offer a few examples, below are several teachings from the *Sayings of the Desert Fathers*[1] on stillness:

- "One living in *hesychia* needs these three things: to fear God without ceasing, to intercede with patient endurance, and not to release his heart from being mindful of God."
- "*Hesychia* is good for this reason: because it does not see that which is harmful and the mind does not absorb what it did not see. That which is not lodged in the mind does not stir a memory through imagination; that which does not stir the memory does not excite the passion, and when the passion is not excited, there is profound calm and great peace within."
- "He who is devoted to *hesychia* remains invulnerable to the darts of the enemy, but he who is involved with multitudes is continually getting wounded. For [having a bad temper], when it is at rest, becomes more gentle; and desire, when it is in *hesychia*, becomes accustomed to react more mild in accordance with reason. When not being stirred up, every passion simply progresses gently to what is more moderate and later completely ceases, in time forgetting its own activity; and then there remain unimportant memories of things since the passionate disposition has withdrawn."

- "The beginning of evils is distraction."
- "A monk ought to acquire *hesychia* for himself in order to be able to count it as nothing even if he suffers physical damage."
- "Unless a person says in his heart, 'I alone and God are in the world,' he will not [find rest].'"

As the above sayings reveal, within the walls of the cell, early desert Christians strived to cultivate a deeper stillness and inner quiet on a day to day basis, longing for a more authentic connection with God, who was active and present with them in solitude. In fact, notice that one of the sayings above even advocates for allowing emotions to run their natural course, with inner experiences simply receding into the background. As monks focused on God, it was almost as if their compulsive, tempting thoughts lost their influence, residing in the background without the ability to distract them from what mattered.

To draw a parallel with present-moment awareness, the "peace of mind" that these desert residents sought emanated from an awareness of God's active, loving presence, surrendering the inner world to him. To focus their attention on one thing at a time—God's presence in the cell by way of reciting scripture—was a central goal, given that they believed that tempting, compulsive thoughts would naturally arise when they were living life within the walls of their quarters. Overall, a sense of peaceful stillness is apparently possible in the Christian life, captured some 1,500 years ago by desert monks who got to know the inner workings of the mind.

In the 21st century, one of the ways silence and stillness are cultivated is through the Jesus Prayer, practiced in a prior chapter and again in a subsequent section of this chapter: "Lord Jesus Christ, Son of God, have mercy on me, a sinner." To be sure, this famous prayer seems to capture the gospel message fully, and can help you to continuously focus on God's presence, calling out to him as you pray to guard your heart so that Jesus' name will begin to repeat itself throughout your day (Coniaris, 1998). In other words, several key ingredients are embedded within the Jesus Prayer.

First, as you recite the prayer ever so slowly and gently, the words begin to sink in. Over time, the powerful words of the prayer are less of a cognitive endeavor, and more of a heartfelt plea to God for mercy and compassion. Second, the actual words, when repeated throughout your day, can help you with sustained attention, focusing on Jesus, rather than ruminative thoughts about the past or worrying thoughts about the future. Differently stated, *hesychia* is cultivated with the Jesus Prayer because you are devoting all of your attention to him, letting go of the tendency to fuse with or avoid distressing inner experiences, which often reside in the background, rather than at the forefront of attention. Finally, with the Jesus Prayer, you are developing the ability to stay rooted in the present moment, devoting yourself to surrendering to his providential care, instead of spending your mental energy warring with depressive or anxiety-related symptoms.

Above all else, the Jesus Prayer can help you with ACT's present-moment awareness process, given the following characteristics:

- Focusing on one thing at a time—Jesus Christ.
- Staying rooted in the present moment, where Jesus is ministering to you and offering you his grace and mercy.
- Allowing your thoughts and feelings to arise organically and naturally drift away, given you are focusing on the words of the prayer, which repeat within your heart.

Stillness and Silence and the Mary Mode
To relate silence and stillness to the Mary mode, reminiscent of Mary sitting at Jesus' feet in the Gospel of Luke, a central ingredient of her yielding posture seemed to involve a quietness that led to the ability to immerse herself in Jesus' world. In other words, from my perspective, to sit at Jesus' feet, focusing exclusively on him, requires the ability to settle into the experience, attending exclusively to what he is saying. Without quieting the mind through a calm, peaceful stillness, focusing on him may pose a challenge, reminiscent of Martha's anxious activity.

Resembling ACT's present-moment awareness, Mary seemed to be able to sit quietly at Jesus' feet, with a calm, patient, yielding posture so as to learn from him. *Hesychia*, therefore, appears to be about surrendering to God, letting go of the tendency to chase or push away the thinking process, gently returning to an awareness of God's presence when you notice your attention has drifted. Whether reciting the Jesus Prayer or quite literally sitting at his feet as he teaches, instructs, and invites you to directly experience the "gospel message," an inner stillness is developed with single-minded attention, reminiscent of the early desert monks who humbly surrendered everything to be with God in the cell.

Stillness and Silence and Emotional Disorders

With emotional disorders, *hesychia* may involve the ability to find a deeper sense of quiet, peace, and stillness, even when difficult thoughts, feelings, and sensations will not go away. Like the early desert Christians' daily experience of the *logismoi*, an inner peace is still possible, even when the mind's distractions will not subside. To cultivate a deeper sense of peace and stillness, monks focused on God's presence, reciting and singing the Psalms as a way to surrender to God's providential care. In a similar vein, stillness in the 21st century requires repeatedly shifting your focus to God's active, loving presence, captured via the Jesus Prayer and other contemplative efforts.

As you learn to recite the Jesus Prayer repeatedly, further explored below, you may begin to develop the ability to shift your focus to God whenever the inner waves begin to crash against the rocks. In other words, pivoting to the lighthouse can help you maintain an awareness of God's presence, even when the storm is at its worst on a dark, cold winter night. As ACT's present-moment awareness process reveals, to be rooted in the here and now, whether relating to the inner or outer world, can help you to relate differently to life's stressors.

By asking Jesus for *mercy*—that is, a compassionate responsiveness—you are shedding your own tendency to get lost in the world of language, letting your mind bully you around and pulling you away from God's loving presence. To stay planted in each moment, crying out to God for him to reveal himself, means you are ameliorating the tendency to lose sight of the task at hand—following Jesus on the path he is leading you down, even while in tremendous psychological pain. Whether drawing from the experience of early monks' single-minded devotion to God as they let go of all their possessions to deepen their relationship with him or adopting Mary's unyielding posture as she attentively listened to Jesus, the strength of stillness lies in the ability to rest in Jesus' presence. Certainly, Jesus' yoke is easy and his burden is light (Matthew 11:30).

Stillness and Silence Metaphors

- Inner stillness is like Noah and his family when they closed the door of the ark, knowing that God was protecting them in spite of the flooding waters that surrounded them (Colombiere, 1980). Similarly, I can accept distressing thoughts, feelings, and sensations, knowing that God is directing my inner world, in order to be more aware of his creation and my life within it.

- Inner stillness is like Moses leading God's chosen people across the Red Sea, knowing they were safe from the water on both sides, which was visible but could not harm them. Even though I experience difficult thoughts, feelings, and sensations, which might not go away, I can be at peace in knowing that God is directing my paths and guiding my inner world.

- Inner stillness is like Jesus appearing to the disciples after he rose from the dead, resulting in his followers having confidence that death had been overcome. Even though they knew they had a difficult road ahead, Jesus' promises had been fulfilled, giving them added hope and encouragement. In my own life, despite my depressive or anxiety-related symptoms, I can cultivate an inner quiet, knowing that Jesus offers me his grace and mercy, reconciling me to God through his atonement.

- Inner stillness is like Jesus tempted in the desert for 40 days. Although the devil tried to distract him, he remained firmly focused on God's promises in scripture, keeping his attention on the words of the Bible. In my own life, I will experience a wide variety of distressing thoughts and feelings; yet, I can still stay focused on God, leading to the ability to live out my virtues from moment to moment.

Exercise: "Staying Put" in Your Cell

For this exercise, I would like for you to imagine you are a desert monk in the 5th century, residing in your cell. During this time, you are consistently distracted with tempting thoughts and overwhelming feelings. In order to shift your focus, you begin to gently recite a short phrase from the Psalms. In particular, you slowly start to repeat Psalm 28:7:

- "The Lord is my strength and my shield; my heart trusts in him, and he helps me."

As you recite the verse, begin to focus on God's presence, with an inner stillness. In other words, try to remain calm, without striving towards any other state. You are focusing on cultivating an inner quiet, given that you are making no effort to turn up or turn down the volume of your mind. Rather, you are solely devoted to absorbing Psalm 28:7, which helps you acknowledge God's presence within the four walls of your cell.

Whenever you notice that you are distracted with a thought or feeling, just acknowledge that you have been sidetracked, before compassionately returning to reciting Psalm 28:7. If possible, pay particular attention to the promises embedded in the passage, with God serving as a shield and source of strength. In fact, because God helps you in your time of need, you can trust him in an uncompromising, unwavering manner.

For about ten minutes, continue to recite the Psalm, absorbing its message as you cultivate a present-focused attentiveness, yielding to God's presence. Whenever you notice you are distracted in your cell, return to God's presence, over and over again. Begin to notice the pattern that emerges, with your thoughts and feelings swimming beneath the surface, coming above water to make an appearance, then dipping back into the waters of your mind, over and over again.

Once you are finished with the exercise, please reflect on what it was like for you. In particular, try to consider the role that a present-moment awareness of God—captured by slowly and gently reciting a specific verse in the Psalms—played in helping you let go of the tendency to chase or push away your distracting thoughts and feelings. How, if at all, can this focused attention help you rest in God's presence throughout your day, cultivating a calm stillness because of your awareness of him?

_____

_____

_____

_____

_____

_____

_____

_____

_____

Exercise: Floating on the Ark with Inner Stillness and Silence[2]

In this exercise, I would like for you to imagine that God has chosen you to go with Noah on the ark. As you close the door to the ark, watching the rain pour down, you know that you will be safe within the walls of the gigantic wooden vessel. In other words, although there is chaos outside, you are able to rest, knowing God is sovereign.

On the ark, of course, there are many animals (two of every kind, to be sure). Because you are sharing space with a wide variety of God's creatures, your environment inevitably smells, and is most certainly loud and distracting. However, because you are safely floating on the water, surrendering your life to God, you have an inner calm. In fact, there is a significant amount of chaos both inside and outside of the ark; yet, your soul feels well rested.

As you notice all of the distractions—the storm outside and the animals inside—you are able to return gently to an awareness of God's presence, knowing that he has chosen you to take the next step forward with the human race, which is his creation. Because of this awareness of God's providence, you can be still and quiet, resting in his presence. Again, based on the notion that God is guiding the ark, you can remain focused on him, rather than the distractions around you.

In the space that follows, see if you can reflect on this exercise, writing down some of your thoughts about the experience. Questions to consider:

1 What might it have been like for Noah and his family on the ark, trusting in God's providence in spite of the uncertainty and chaos that surrounded them?
2 In your own life, is it possible to cultivate an inner calm, reminiscent of being in the boat, safely waiting for the waters to recede, given that God is in control of your life?
3 How can you extend this awareness of God's active, loving presence to daily life, based on this understanding that stillness and silence in the presence of God can bring inner peace, even when the storms of life are all around you?
4 How, if at all, does the story of Noah parallel monks' commitment to staying in the cell, pursuing *hesychia* in spite of their likely hunger, tempting thoughts, and boredom?

_____

_____

_____

_____

_____

_____

_____

_____

_____

_____

Exercise: The Jesus Prayer

Within this exercise, I would like for you to first read a few verses in scripture to better understand some of the possible scriptural influences for the Jesus Prayer. To begin, please read the following two sections of scripture, one in Luke (18:10–13) and the other in 1 Thessalonians (5:16–18):

- "Two men went up to the temple to pray, one a Pharisee and the other a tax collector. The Pharisee stood by himself and prayed: 'God, I thank you that I am not like other people—robbers, evildoers, adulterers—or even like this tax collector. I fast twice a week and give a tenth of all I get.' But the tax collector stood at a distance. He would not even look up to heaven, but beat his breast and said, 'God, have mercy on me, a sinner.'"
- "Rejoice always, pray continually, give thanks in all circumstances; for this is God's will for you in Christ Jesus."

In these two sections of scripture, a tax collector cried out to God for mercy, and Paul instructed his audience to pray constantly, no matter what life experiences arose.

Therefore, for this exercise, see if you can recite the Jesus Prayer throughout your day, praying and thanking God for his mercy, no matter what happens. Whether you experience inner or outer distress, continue to shift your focus towards God, cultivating a deeper stillness and silence in his presence. As you recite the prayer—"Lord Jesus

Christ, Son of God, have mercy on me, a sinner"—remember to let the words penetrate your heart, deepening your ability to rest in him.

At the end of the day, after reciting the Jesus Prayer, see if you can write down some of your reactions. What was the experience like for you, especially given your focus was on Jesus throughout the day?

_____

_____

_____

_____

_____

_____

_____

_____

_____

Exercise: Centering Prayer with the Breath[3]

For this 20-minute exercise, I would like you to build on your previous efforts to learn centering prayer with a phrase. Now, I would like for you to deepen your awareness of God's active, loving presence—an inner stillness and silence—by connecting to your breathing. This form of contemplative practice, certainly, is embedded within several world religions, including Buddhism and Christianity. In either case, noticing the breath is important because it offers a window into the present moment, anchoring you to the here and now. Since you are always breathing, without having to do anything, the breath can be a way to deepen your ability to rest at this moment.

For Christians, the breath is important because it can represent the "breath of life" that God poured into Adam in Genesis 2:7. Within contemplative practice, you can begin to recognize that God controls your breathing, offering the gift of life to you. In other words, because of God's grace and mercy, you have been born into this world, with the opportunity to live each moment in relationship with him.

To begin this practice, get into a comfortable position, closing your eyes to let go of all the visual distractions in your environment. When you are ready, begin to notice that you are breathing, paying attention to your breath in one part of your body. For example, you might want to pay attention to the breath going in and out of your mouth, especially where your breath is felt on your lips. Or, you might prefer to notice your abdomen expanding and contracting, without any added effort on your part.

Nevertheless, just notice your breathing, letting go of all of your efforts to control your breathing in any way. After all, God gave you the "breath of life," and is lovingly offering you the ability to walk with him in his proverbial garden. Therefore, just notice, without fixing or striving to make your experience different in any way. Approach the exercise with a calm, quiet stillness, gently relinquishing your own tendency to want to control what happens at this moment.

At a certain point, you will recognize that you have been distracted by a thought or feeling, which pulls you away from your awareness of your breathing. When this happens, just acknowledge what led you astray, before slowly returning to God's gift—your breathing. You might be distracted each and every minute during the exercise, which is perfectly okay, and lets you know that your mind is busy and active. Reminiscent of Noah waiting patiently and calmly on the ark, see if you can just acknowledge the storms of the mind, before returning to an awareness of God's presence via your God-given breathing pattern.

Exercise: *Lectio Divina*

In addition to centering prayer, *lectio divina*, translated as "divine reading," is a way to cultivate a deeper awareness of God's active, loving presence. Within the practice, there are four basic steps (adapted from Benner, 2010):

- *Lectio*: read the chosen passage in scripture, focusing on absorbing the verse.
- *Meditatio*: reflect on the passage that was just read, attempting to discern God's intentions for the verse in the present moment.
- *Oratio*: respond to God's word, offering thanks for your time spent with him.
- *Contemplatio*: rest in God's active, loving presence, yielding to his providential care.

If possible, see if you can select your own passage to ponder, trusting that God will guide you through the process as you focus on him. From there, try to move slowly through each stage, completing the exercise in about 20 minutes. When you are finished, use the boxes below to reflect on the experience, with the main goal being to cultivate an inner stillness and present-moment awareness of God, relying on the Bible to do so.

		Comments
Passage in Scripture		
	Read	
	Reflect	
	Respond	
	Rest	

Exercise: Reflections on a Mountain Lake[4]

In this exercise, you will continue to develop your ability to focus on God in the present moment, cultivating an inner quiet and silence along the way. In particular, this exercise will focus on deepening your awareness of God's active, loving presence by practicing stillness, drawing from one of God's most beautiful creations—a mountain lake—to capture stillness. To use this metaphor, *hesychia* is like a still, clear lake that has no waves or ripples, vividly reflecting the bright, spacious sky overhead.

In order to begin, I would like for you to sit in a comfortable position, closing your eyes and sitting up straight in a supportive chair. Place your feet firmly on the floor. When you are ready, begin to imagine you are sitting in a beach chair on the shore of a still, clear lake. On this crisp, bright summer afternoon, the wind is blowing; yet, the environment is extremely quiet. As you notice your surroundings, you are especially moved by the calmness and stillness of the lake. In fact, you can see—with crystal-clear precision—the sky shining off of the glassy mountain lake. As you let go of all fidgeting and restless activity, you again notice that the air is blowing, the leaves are moving about, and the sky is reflecting off the surface, which almost looks like a mirror.

In each passing moment, you continue to return to the lake's surface, which brilliantly reflects God's creation—the beautiful sky. From time to time, your attention is pulled away by flocks of birds in the air and small airplanes jettisoning across the sky. What is more, just beneath the surface, there are fish actively swimming about. Yet, you quickly return to the stillness of the surface. There is nothing else you need to do, other than watch the calm of the lake, which reflects the blue sky above.

Now, try to cultivate a similar stillness within your inner world, letting go of all efforts to move or fidget via chasing or pushing away thoughts, feelings, or sensations. Instead, like the surface of the lake, your job is to simply let God's glory permeate your inner world, shining through as you yield to his active, loving presence. Reminiscent of the birds and airplanes, you just let your thoughts, feelings, and sensations move through your inner dimensions.

Regardless of the movements occurring inside, like fish just beneath the surface of the water, you are quiet and still, allowing God to reflect his glory, similar to the blue sky reflecting on the lake. Again, your job is to simply remain still, functioning like the glassy surface—just reflecting God's glory, allowing the inner world to do what it will do, reminiscent of the birds and fish in nature on a bright, sunny day within a mountain community.

Sit in this silent stillness for about ten minutes, remembering that your job is to simply let go of all efforts at striving, fixing, or problem solving. Instead, like the lake, just remain still, so that God's glory can shine on your proverbial lake surface. As this exercise comes to a close, see if you can write down some of your thoughts:

- What was it like to just watch the lake, which mirrored the sky?
- How did you do allowing your thoughts, feelings, and sensations to run their natural course, just focusing on allowing God's glory to shine?

- How might you continue to be still, using silence to cultivate *hesychia* throughout your day, especially when you are distracted by unpleasant thoughts, feelings, and sensations?

_____

_____

_____

_____

_____

_____

_____

_____

_____

_____

Conclusion

In this chapter, you explored ACT's present-moment awareness, which can help you to ameliorate the tendency to be lost in the mind, preoccupied with the past or the future. Because life unfolds in the here and now, finding ways to anchor you to the present moment can be helpful for value-based living. As a parallel, early desert Christians attempted to cultivate a deeper sense of stillness and silence, focusing on God's presence in order to let go of the distractions and temptations they encountered in the cell. With emotional disorders, there can be a tendency to get distracted with unpleasant thoughts, feelings, and sensations, ruminating about the past or worrying about the future. When this happens, *hesychia* can help you turn your attention to God, acknowledging your inner distress before attending to his active, loving presence.

In terms of the actual exercises, you were able to practice several contemplative strategies, learn about a variety of biblical metaphors that seem to capture a calm, still inner experience, and apply what you have learned to daily living. In the next chapter, you will focus on the contemplative self, which can help you to better understand the importance of a spiritual, intuitive part of your sense of self, reaching out to God experientially, rather than through words and language. After the next chapter, you will learn about ACT's values and committed action processes, drawing a parallel with virtue-based action and following Jesus in the Christian tradition.

Notes

1 The quotes in this section are from Wortley (2012). Used with permission.
2 This exercise is inspired by Colombiere (1980), who argued that peace and happiness are possible—regardless of the innumerable inner and outer events that lead to psychological and spiritual pain—because God is sovereign and infinitely wise, offering a loving response and guidance in the midst of suffering.
3 See Frenette (2012) for a review of the role that breathing plays in centering prayer. For an overview of mindfulness of breathing, see Williams, Teasdale, Segal, and Kabat-Zinn (2007).
4 This exercise is inspired by a quote from St. Joseph the Hesychast, "The aim was *hesychia*, quiet, the calm through the whole man that is like a still pool of water, capable of reflecting the sun" (quoted in Chumley, 2014, p. 2).

References

Benner, D. (2010). *Opening to God: Lectio Divina and Life as Prayer.* Downers Grove, IL: InterVarsity Press.

Chryssavgis, J. (2008). *In the Heart of the Desert: The Spirituality of the Desert Fathers and Mothers.* Bloomington, IN: World Wisdom, Inc.

Chumley, N. (2014). *Be Still and Know: God's Presence and Silence.* Minneapolis, MN: Augsburg Fortress.

Colombiere, C. (1980). *Trustful Surrender to Divine Providence: The Secret of Peace and Happiness.* Charlotte, NC: TAN Books.

Coniaris, A. (1998). *Philokalia: The Bible of Orthodox Spirituality.* Minneapolis, MN: Light & Life Publishing Company.

Frenette, D. (2012). *The Path of Centering Prayer: Deepening your Experience of God.* Boulder, CO: Sounds True, Inc.

Harmless, W. (2004). *Desert Christians: An Introduction to the Literature of Early Monasticism.* New York: Oxford University Press.

Harris, R. (2009). *ACT Made Simple: An Easy-to-Read Primer on Acceptance and Commitment Therapy.* Oakland, CA: New Harbinger Publications, Inc.

Hayes, S., Strosahl, K., & Wilson, K. (2012). *Acceptance and Commitment Therapy: The Process and Practice of Mindful Change* (2nd ed.). New York: The Guilford Press.

Stewart, C. (2015). *World of the Desert Fathers: Stories and Sayings from the Anonymous Series of the Apophthegmata Patrum.* Oxford: SLG Press.

Williams, M., Teasdale, J., Segal, Z., & Kabat-Zinn, J. (2007). *The Mindful Way Through Depression: Freeing Yourself from Chronic Unhappiness.* New York: The Guilford Press.

Wortley, J. (2012). *The Book of Elders: Sayings of the Desert Fathers.* Trappist, KY: Cistercian Publications.

Chapter 6: The Observing Self and Awareness of the Contemplative Self

Introduction

In this chapter, you will read about ACT's observing self process, which can help you relate to your inner experiences with a bit more openness, disengaging from an overreliance on them so as to follow your values flexibly. Specifically, the observing self is a way to take a different perspective, viewing unpleasant thoughts, feelings, and sensations with distance and detached awareness. Similar to watching boats float by as you stand on a dock, the observing self can allow you to experience psychological pain with a more curious, non-judgmental attitude, pivoting towards value-based living in the process.

Conversely, ACT's verbal self is the storied self, relying on words and the world of language to determine both who you are and your course of action. When overly relying on the verbal self, you may find that you have a hard time living out your values, since your mind can be very convincing about what you can and cannot do. By pivoting towards an awareness of the observing self, you may be able to improve your ability to intentionally go where you would like, reliant on values to guide your life, rather than a predetermined narrative that is keeping you stuck.

For early desert Christians, the *nous*—defined as the "eye of the soul," contemplative self, or heart (Chumley, 2014)—captures the part of the soul that experiences God directly, rather than relying on reason or logic. In fact, in the *Philokalia*, a collection of contemplative writings that date back to the 4th century, a wide variety of authors illuminated this distinction. Therefore, similar to the observing self, contemplatives throughout the ages have let go of the tendency to solely use language and words when resting in God's presence. Instead, cultivating a deeper union with God involves sometimes relating to him in a wordless state, reaching out to him in love, rather than knowledge (Bangley, 2006). Stated differently, detaching from a preoccupation with the *logismoi* can be helpful to experience God directly, like keenly observing a beautiful waterfall with your very own eyes, rather than merely viewing a photograph or postcard of a waterfall in some distant, far away land.

Throughout the chapter, you will explore the different facets of this part of the Christian self, practicing exercises and strategies to relate to God with *apophatic* prayer. When applied to emotional disorders, deepening your awareness of the *nous* may help you let go of the tendency to overly rely on thoughts, feelings, and sensations in the Christian life. Rather, allowing these inner experiences to run their natural course, watching them from a safe distance, can help you rest in God, beyond words and images.

To begin to change the *nous, metanoia* is required—heading in a different direction, letting go of attachments to distracting thoughts and feelings in order to yield to God's active, loving presence (Amis, 1995). To do this, contemplative prayer can help you begin to walk down the path of a more intimate union with God, transforming the *nous* to be more like Christ. In fact, dating back to the early desert Christians, a central focus in contemplative Christianity has been the transformation of the *nous* to more accurately reflect Jesus' heart (see Nassif, 2012; 1 Corinthians 2:16).[1]

ACT's Observing Self Process
In ACT, there are several ways to view the *self*, which can help you to make sense of your possible struggle with disordered functioning, including the verbal self and observing self (Luoma, Hayes, & Walser, 2007). To begin, the *verbal self* is the part of you that relies on a narrative to define who you are. Drawing from the world of language, this aspect of your sense of self emphasizes the story you tell yourself, based in part on your past. Over time, you begin to write a seemingly coherent narrative that you can heavily rely upon to guide life, drawing from this fixed story to better understand who you are. In fact, in addition to serving as a relatively stable self-concept, you can quickly turn to your verbal self to evaluate situations, solve problems in relationships, and make decisions about major life events. You might even employ the verbal self to establish a set of goals for life, although you may sell yourself short when you overly rely on this predefined narrative about who you are and what you are capable of accomplishing.

Here, of course, you can see that the verbal self can be both helpful and harmful in your ability to live out your values. As an example, you might have a history of trauma, abuse, or neglect in your family-of-origin. Growing up, you may have been repeatedly told you were "worthless" or "useless." Understandably, you might have started to tell yourself a story about who you are, based in part on the messages you received from those around you.

In childhood, it is possible this narrative began to solidify, leading to an adolescence filled with doubt and uncertainty as you grew into an independent person. As you matured into adulthood, you might have fused with this story, which now defines who you are and the directions you take in life. Without slowing down to question this language-based narrative, you may have come to the conclusion that there is no way you are going to be able to live the life you want, especially since you "know for certain" that you lack worth.

Conversely, the observing self is a self-perspective for watching this story unfold within your mind, without concluding that the narrative is definitively "true." Stated differently, there is a part of *you* that has watched this story being written since you began to form memories and draw conclusions with language-based evaluations. Certainly, there is an author behind the pen, watching the words form as they are written on the page. This is the part of you that watches your thoughts, feelings, and sensations, safely noticing what is happening from a distance, given that you are much more than these impermanent inner experiences.

If possible, think about all the descriptions you carry around about yourself, recognizing there is a *you* that is staring at each of them, transcending their seemingly inevitable influence. Instead of assuming you "know" you are "worthless," try to notice there is a part of you that recognizes these words on the page of this workbook, with a sense of distance. When this understanding is applied to emotional disorders, you can work towards observing your inner world with more open curiosity, reminiscent of going on a jungle safari.

See if you can imagine planning to go on an African safari for about a year, eagerly anticipating the trip and looking forward to watching all of the wild life, with a sense of awe and excitement. When your airplane lands on the African continent, your very first thought is that you want to go on the animal safari. When you get there, you climb into the jeep, with the tour guide steadily driving the vehicle to your destination.

Arriving at your destination, you quickly notice a family of giraffes, along with some trees in the distance and a small lake. Taking in the scenery, you are taken aback by the beauty. As you continue on, driving around the African landscape, you notice a wide variety of animals and vegetation. Yet, throughout the experience, you are able to recognize that *you* are not the animals or vegetation. There is a *you* that is watching the experience, realizing you are much more than these incoming sensory experiences. In fact, observing a pack of lions in the distance, you would never say to yourself, "I am one of those lions."

To draw a parallel, the inner world is not unlike watching wildlife. Over time, you will observe all kinds of "animals," including pleasant and unpleasant thoughts and feelings, none of which fully captures the *you* that is noticing. Although you might have a pesky "I'm worthless" thought, reminiscent of a fly circling around your face, you can recognize there is a *you* that is noticing the nagging thought. Based on this realization, inner experiences become less overwhelming and scary; given that you are safely tucked away in the back seat of a jeep, watching God's creatures move about within the arid African landscape can be experienced with more curiosity and awe.

Taking a step back to notice there is a *you* behind the camera of life, looking through the lens to actually snap the pictures from moment to moment, can be helpful for a few reasons. To start, connecting to the observing self can allow you to defuse from a story that is keeping you stuck, letting go of the narrative you may have written when you were very young. Rather than letting this sense of self define you, there is a vast, open space to just notice this is one of many thoughts that float around in your mind. Reminiscent of looking in an old shoebox of finger paintings you made in grade school some 20 years ago, you might simply say to yourself, "How precious. I tried so hard. The picture in no way, though, captures reality, given my limited understanding and vantage point." Similarly, you may be able to move in the direction of thanking your mind for the old stories, but recognize they are outdated, failing to capture the *you* that is living in present day society.

Moreover, when you can begin to connect to the observing self, avoidance is much less likely. Given you have some extra space to simply watch, inner distress can be gently and compassionately noticed, without feeling forced to respond because your thoughts and feelings are definitively you. Rather, you can take note of what is unfolding, before pivoting to value-based living, reminiscent of safely watching a storm from the porch of your house. When observing this storm, you can just watch the lightning, listen to the thunder, and notice that the rain is pouring down, without running inside and slamming the door shut in anticipation of being sucked into the passing, impermanent event outside.

Interestingly, the early desert Christians described a similar sense of self. However, for these devoted Christians, the contemplative self longed to experience God directly, beyond words and images. In other words, rather than merely serving as a viewpoint, or way to simply notice the inner world, this sense of self was created in God's image to unite with him. As a result, what follows is a review of the *nous*, before transitioning to several exercises to help you deepen your awareness of the contemplative self. Prior to reading about this aspect of the Christian life, though, see if you can write down some characteristics of the storied, verbal self you have created over the years (this will be further developed, too, in a subsequent section of the chapter). Some questions to consider:

- What kinds of descriptions do you use to describe yourself?
- When did these descriptions begin to form, and how do they relate to the story of you?
- What story have you written about yourself?
- How, if at all, does this story guide your relationships?
- How, if at all, does this story guide major decisions you make in life?
- What would life be like if you were able to let go of the grip this story has on you?

_____

_____

_____

_____

_____

_____

_____

Early Desert Christians and the Contemplative Self

For Evagrius Ponticus, a 4th-century desert Christian, the mind can be divided into the *nous*, which connects to God directly and intuitively by way of faith, and the thinking, reasoning mind, which employs concepts and logic to understand him (Laird, 2006). During contemplative prayer, Christians encounter God beyond words and logic (Harmless, 2004), reminiscent of the distinction between the verbal and observing self in ACT.

To offer a fitting example, instantaneously recognizing your child's laugh is very different from relying on concepts to know *about* how your child laughs. This distinction, of course, can be applied to your relationship with God, too. In Evagrius' writings, he presented his notion of "pure prayer," which does not involve employing words or images to cultivate a deeper union with God. From this perspective, developing a more intimate relationship with God involves a direct experience of him, beyond the use of language (Harmless, 2004).

Within the *Philokalia*, the *nous* is defined as the "eye of the soul," heart, or center of being, relying on spiritual intuition to know something directly, rather than using concepts or reason (Chumley, 2014; Coniaris, 2004). Conversely, *dianoia* describes your ability to use reason and logic to understand the world around you, including your relationship with God (Smith, 2013). This distinction, of course, can help you to make sense of different ways of experiencing God, whether through silent, wordless prayer or studying scripture and making sense of Christian theology, thinking through different concepts within Christian orthodoxy.

In the contemplative tradition, you have the contemplative self. This "self" longs to connect to God directly, beyond words and reason. You also have the reasoning, thinking mind (which is sort of an outer layer, surrounding your core self). The latter is most certainly useful for a variety of activities in your Christian faith, including studying the Bible.

For instance, you might typically think about God on a daily basis. However, you may struggle to rest in God's presence, transcending your reliance on words to describe him. Because of this, contemplative prayer can help you to directly experience God, letting go of the tendency to use the verbal self as a way to deepen your relationship with him.

As one final example, imagine sitting in silence with a close friend, eating breakfast together at the dining room table of your home. In this moment, you look up at your friend, who is eating her cereal. Instantly, you have a sense that you know her, letting go of the need to think through the "facts" *about* your relationship with her. Having this direct experience, you find no need to access memories to prove your friend is trustworthy or special; rather, you intuitively know her, and can eat in silence, enjoying the time spent together.

This example can help you better understand the need to cultivate an intuitive, direct experience of God, knowing him without having to convince yourself he is active and present. Instead, you are able to truly see God, sitting in silence with him in a wordless, imageless prayer state. Over time, you may come to especially appreciate this union with God, reminiscent of sitting at the breakfast table with a friend, relinquishing the need to use words to describe your bonded closeness.

The Contemplative Self as a "Little Radio"

Within the *Philokalia*, a series of contemplative writings in the Eastern Orthodox tradition that date back to the early desert Christians, the *nous* represents the intuitive self, directly experiencing the world, beyond logic and reason. To be sure, the *nous* has recently been described as a way to "perceive God's voice and presence," a sort of "little radio" that senses God, beyond mere thinking and feeling (Mathewes-Green, 2009, p. 39).

Unfortunately, though, tempting thoughts (i.e., the *logismoi*) and powerful emotions (i.e., passions) can distract the contemplative self (Mathewes-Green, 2009). Therefore, within contemplative Christianity, the Jesus Prayer is commonly used to cultivate a deeper awareness of his presence, letting go of distracting thoughts by repeatedly shifting the focus back to the famous saying: "Lord Jesus Christ, Son of God, have mercy on me, a sinner." Over time, you may begin to recognize God's presence in everyday life, hearing his "still small voice," like a radio station playing a tune you instantly know and love.

Sayings from the *Philokalia* on the *Nous*

To further explore the *nous*, below are some teachings on this intuitive part of the self from the *Philokalia*,[2] which seems to have grown in popularity in recent years, beyond its reach within the Orthodox tradition:

- "I entreat you not to leave your heart unguarded, as long as you are in the body. Just as a farmer cannot feel confident about the crop growing in his fields, because he does not know what will happen to it before it is stored away in his granary, so a man should not leave his heart unguarded as long as he still has breath in his nostrils. Up to his last breath he cannot know what passion will attack him; as long as he breathes, therefore, he must not leave his heart unguarded, but should at every moment pray to God for his help and mercy."
- "A heart that has been completely emptied of mental images gives birth to divine, mysterious intellections that sport within like fish and dolphins in a calm sea. The sea is fanned by a soft wind, the heart's depth by the Holy Spirit."
- "At every hour and moment let us guard the heart with all diligence from thoughts that obscure the soul's mirror; for in that mirror Jesus Christ, the wisdom and power of God the Father (1 Corinthians 1:24), is typified and luminously reflected."
- "A true sanctuary, even before the life to come, is a heart free from distractive thoughts and energized by the Spirit, for all is done and said there spiritually."

In these quotes, notice there is a theme of guarding the heart (which includes the *nous*). In other words, thoughts and feelings can get in the way of a direct, intuitive experience of God; therefore, staying on guard (i.e., watchfulness) is a way to rely on the spiritual self to commune with him. Thoughts and feelings, to be sure, are part of your experience, but make up a sort of outer layer, at times covering over and distracting you from an awareness of God's presence (revealed via the *nous*).

Above all else, watchfulness can be helpful so as to preserve the space between the *logismoi* and heart/*nous*, reminiscent of the verbal/observing self distinction in ACT. To detach from an overreliance on thoughts and feelings, especially when they get in the way of virtuous living, can move you in the direction of following Jesus as he guides your paths. In turn, you can begin to trust he is active and present as your life unfolds from moment to moment.

The Contemplative Self and the Mary Mode

To relate the contemplative self to the story of Mary and Martha in the gospel of Luke, Mary sat patiently at the feet of Jesus, possibly letting go of all her distractions as she focused on him. To apply the concept of the *nous* to Mary's experience, sitting at Jesus' feet involves letting go of the tendency to use reason and words to make sense of your encounter with him. Alternatively, you are experiencing Jesus directly.

In your prayer life, relating to God in an imageless, wordless state means taking a break from your reliance upon the *dianoia* to make sense of God. Rather, resting at Jesus' feet, you are intuitively experiencing him, reminiscent of recognizing your mother's voice in childhood as she calls you home from an illuminated porch because it is dark outside. This direct experience, of course, seems to have relevance for how you relate to your depressive or anxiety-related symptoms, which will be explored next.

For a brief moment, try to imagine what it might be like to sit at Jesus' feet, consistent with Mary in Luke's Gospel account. Try to let go of the tendency to make sense of the experience with thoughts and reason. Instead, absorb the encounter, directly receiving his words and presence.

The Contemplative Self and Emotional Disorders

When you are struggling with depressive and anxiety-related symptoms, you may find it is incredibly difficult to tune into the "little radio," which is God's "still small voice" inviting you to directly, intuitively experience him (Mathewes-Green, 2009). Reminiscent of both ACT's verbal self and *dianoia*, your mind might try to problem solve or reason its way out of your current symptoms, convinced it "knows" who you are in your relationship with others and God. When this happens, the "little radio" may fade away into the background, reminiscent of light classical music playing in the room next door, drowned out by the thunder and rain just outside of your bedroom window.

Yet, watchfulness and the Jesus Prayer can help you to employ the *nous* to have a direct experience of God, sort of like "turning up the volume" to clearly hear the compact disc playing Mozart from the other side of the wall. As you learn to watch the inner world unfold, repeatedly returning to the Jesus Prayer, the *nous* is able to more accurately perceive God's voice, directly receiving his message and sensing his active, loving presence. Of course, your direct experience of God is not likely to be delivered as a clear, audible voice that comes through parting clouds in the sky; rather, your direct experience of God may involve simply resting in his presence, relating to him beyond thoughts and feelings.

As you learn to just watch the inner world, you may be able to let go of the tendency to rely on a storied, fused sense of self to guide your actions. Relating to your inner world with more tentativeness and detachment, recognizing there is a you that is watching your distracting thoughts, can help you pivot towards a direct relationship with God, following Jesus in the process. When applying the *nous* to emotional disorders, you may find peace in relinquishing an over-reliance on the thinking mind, which can exacerbate psychological pain, especially when you cannot fully eliminate the *logismoi*. This understanding, to be sure, is also captured in a recent psychotherapy approach that uses mindfulness to relate differently to emotional disorders.

The Contemplative Self and the "Being" Mode

Given that the *nous* seeks out a direct experience of God, letting go of reason and discursive thinking, it may be helpful to explore the overlap between the contemplative self mentioned in this chapter and the "being" mode of the mind, elucidated in mindfulness-based cognitive therapy (MBCT). In MBCT, which is a recently developed acceptance-based therapy that employs mindfulness to ameliorate emotional disorders, there is a distinction between the "doing" and "being" mode of the mind (Segal, Williams, & Teasdale, 2012).

Briefly discussed in a prior chapter, the "doing" mode involves trying to "fix" inner experiences, reliant upon problem solving and reasoning in the process. In other words, discursive thought is employed, which often ends up exacerbating inner pain, given that most distressing thoughts, feelings, and sensations cannot be eliminated with sheer mental effort. When in the "doing" mode, the mind is frequently preoccupied with the past or future—searching, scanning, and troubleshooting.

On the other hand, the "being" mode is rooted in the present moment, letting go of the tendency to use language, reason, and problem solving to think your way out of inner distress. Rather, the "being" mode, by way of mindfulness meditation, can help you accept impermanent thoughts, feelings, and sensations, allowing them to run their natural course in order to avoid added suffering.

In the "being" mode, you are directly experiencing what is going on inside, without employing *dianoia* to sort things out.

The purpose of transitioning from the "doing" mode (which is helpful when problem solving challenges in the outer world, but not responding to inner events) to the "being" mode (which is useful for relating to unpleasant inner events with more curiosity and compassion, allowing them to naturally move about) is to learn to live life again. In turn, you can let go of the tendency to wait on the "sidelines of life" for your symptoms to go away. In a similar vein, the *nous* relies on direct experiences to discern what is true, relinquishing your own efforts to employ discursive thought to know God during moments of contemplation. Thus, reciting the Jesus Prayer can help you to shift from "doing" to "being," resting in God's loving arms, beyond your own understanding of what is unfolding in the inner world (Proverbs 3:5).

Exercise: Directly Experiencing God

In the space that follows, see if you can identify a key moment in your life that involved directly, intuitively experiencing God, letting go of reason and discursive thought to make sense of your relationship with him. If you can, describe the event, along with your reactions to the encounter. Also, try to describe how, if at all, having more of these intuitive, direct experiences can help you in your daily relationship with God, letting go of the tendency to lean on discursive thinking to follow him and hear his voice. Finally, how can these types of experiences—developed with contemplation and the Jesus Prayer—help you shift from the "doing" mode of the mind to the "being" mode, resting in God's presence without needing to fix, problem solve, or reason your way out of distressing inner experiences?

_____

_____

_____

_____

_____

_____

_____

_____

_____

_____

Below are several metaphors that can help you make sense of the contemplative self, including the *nous/dianoia* distinction. Considering these metaphors can help you to better prepare for the exercises in subsequent parts of this chapter.

The Contemplative Self Metaphors

- The contemplative self is like spending time alone with God, the physician, in silence. God is like the doctor who is treating me in the examination room, actively at work. As he intervenes, I can sit still, trusting he is doing what needs to be done. My thoughts and feelings are like people in the waiting room next door, impatiently grumbling and demanding to come in because it is "their turn" (see Mathewes-Green, 2009).

- The contemplative self is like walking on the beach with God, directly experiencing his presence, beyond words. My thoughts and feelings are like the waves in the ocean, crashing against the shore. I can just let them be, without trying to do anything with them, returning to my immediate experience of God as I walk with him.

- The contemplative self is like experiencing God's presence as I hike in the mountains, having a direct encounter, beyond words. At times, I notice there are airplanes above, flying by, which pulls me out of my intuitive awareness of him. When this happens, I can just acknowledge the planes are overhead, and return to an awareness of God's active, loving presence. Rather than building an airport in the mountains for these planes to land, fusing with them within my inner world, I can just acknowledge them from a safe distance (see Coniaris, 1998).

- The contemplative self is like being made in God's image to enjoy a special relationship with him, consistent with the Genesis account of creation, directly encountering him, beyond words and reason. Whenever I notice that distracting, compulsive thoughts pull me away from this special relationship, which I was designed for, I can simply acknowledge them, before returning to an awareness of his active, loving presence (see Smith, 2013).

- The contemplative self is like watching a beautiful waterfall in nature, directly absorbing the experience, rather than viewing the encounter through the lens of a camera (which represents my thoughts), relying on a photograph with an 'image' of the God-given event.

Exercise: Getting to Know My Storied Self

With this exercise, try to jot down the "story" that you have written about your life (building on the previous exercise), identifying some of the key ingredients. Reminiscent of watching a Hollywood movie, try to capture the plot, including the central players and themes. In your "story," see if you can identify the "good guys" and "bad guys," including the starring or supporting role that you play. If possible, try to consider where this story came from, including whether it was a script that was handed to you or if you were the head writer. If you can, try to be as succinct as possible, reminiscent of reading about the movie on the back of a DVD cover.

_____

_____

_____

_____

_____

_____

_____

_____

Now, if you can, try to imagine what it might be like to just watch the movie, with a sense of detachment and curiosity. Yet, rather than going with a friend to a local movie theatre, you are viewing the movie premiere with God, who will serve as the film critic. Given that you know he is sovereign, infinitely wise, and benevolent, you will be unable to personally offer a final evaluation of your own film; rather, God certainly knows all of the angles, and will be providing a write-up of what he sees in your movie screening.

As the film concludes, though, you realize God has not been taking notes, and is not preparing to give you a point-by-point account of your film. Rather, God just sits in silence with you in the theater as the final credits roll. In turn, you have an overwhelming sense of being loved by him, without needing to do anything else to alter or improve the finished product. As your time with God concludes, he slowly leans over, gently whispering to you that you are a new creation in him (2 Corinthians 5:17), and that your "movie" by no means captures who you are. In fact, God gently reminds you to keep your eyes on him, remembering that the most important part of your movie screening is your unique relationship with him as your creator. As you walk out of the theatre, you begin to see your movie with a bit more detachment, letting go of the tendency to believe it reflects *all* of you. With added confidence, you are able to rest in God, allowing him to define your life, rather than a movie from your past playing on the big screen.

A few questions to consider:

- What might it be like to let God be the only one to judge your "movie," recognizing that he offers you grace and mercy as the one and only critic of your life?
- In other words, can you simply watch your movie, without picking up a pen to evaluate its contents yourself?
- Moving forward, how can you possibly view some of your most distracting thoughts and feelings like a "movie," letting go of the tendency to judge its contents?
- How, if possible, can you focus primarily on cultivating a deeper relationship with God, recognizing you are a new creation in Christ (2 Corinthians 5:17), letting go of the tendency to overly attach to your storied self?

Exercise: Setting Down the Camera to Look Up at Jesus
In this exercise, try to imagine that you are going to travel back in time to the 1st century, somehow presented with the opportunity to go to the house of Mary and Martha to dine with Jesus (Luke 10:

38–42). Given you have planned out this trip beforehand, you eagerly pack a bag, which includes a brand new camera for taking pictures. In fact, one of the things you most look forward to is taking pictures with Jesus, posing with him in order to hold onto the moment, possibly posting snapshots on social media when you return.

As you arrive in your time machine, you use your printed out directions to get you to the house. Knocking on the door, you pull out your camera, placing the strap around your neck in anticipation of seeing Jesus, your Lord and Savior. As Martha welcomes you in, you start taking pictures, one after another, anxiously wanting to pose with Jesus in a variety of different ways. Although you are grateful for the opportunity—in fact, Jesus is extremely accommodating and patient with you—you begin to realize that something is missing.

Suddenly, a light bulb goes off in your head. Your precious time with Jesus is being wasted on photographs, and you are not directly experiencing him. In other words, you are spending all of your time looking through the lens of a camera, rather than directly getting to know Jesus Christ. When this realization occurs, you quickly set down your camera, and sit at Jesus' feet, right next to Mary.

Now, you are staring intently at Jesus, ready to experience his presence, letting go of the tendency to filter your experience through a cheap camera lens. To be sure, you are no longer interested in the "perfect" picture, choosing to directly soak up all that Jesus has to offer. As each moment ticks away, you are fully present, eager to truly *know* him, beyond words, images, and, especially, photographs.

When you are finished immersing yourself in Luke's narrative, try to think back to the times in your life that involved relying on your thoughts and feelings to better understand an experience, rather than just being present and alert to each unfolding moment. This might have been an important conversation with someone, rehearsing what you would say next, rather than being alert and responsive, directly absorbing the conversation. Or, this may have been at an important event, such as a marriage or college graduation, getting lost in your mind, rather than letting yourself directly experience what was unfolding.

Finally, try to think back to a time that involved spending time with God; during this encounter with God, though, you found you were lost in your mind, rather than directly experiencing him. This might have been in a quiet moment, or spending time alone with God in nature. In either case, try to recall an instance that involved relying on thoughts or feelings, attaching to a preconceived notion of God, rather than allowing the moment to organically unfold.

Now, see if you can recognize that there is a *you* that was watching all of these experiences unfold, beyond your distracting, compulsive thoughts, attached to assumptions, judgments, and reason. This same *you*, to be sure, is also now completing this exercise, recognizing you are much more than your thoughts and feelings. Although these inner events are part of you, there is a *you* that longs to connect to God on a deeper level, transcending assumptions, categories, and evaluations of your relationship with him.

When you are finished, see if you can write down some of your reflections on the exercise. What might it be like to detach from some of your distracting thoughts and feelings, letting them run their natural course, rather than viewing your experiences through the "lens of a camera" in each passing moment? Can you apply this realization to God, spending time with him in silence, without trying to capture the experience via thoughts and feelings?

_____

_____

_____

_____

_____

_____

_____

_____

Exercise: Letting Go of the False Self

Another way of making sense of the distinction between the verbal and observing self comes from one of the writings of Pennington (2000), who helped to develop centering prayer in the 1970s. For Pennington, Christians have a true self, found in Christ, along with a false self, which can get in the way of a relationship with him. Therefore, what follows is an exercise to help you distinguish the two, letting go of the verbal false self that may be keeping you stuck in your ability to follow Jesus and recognize God's active, loving presence, which can comfort you and sustain you as you experience psychiatric symptoms.

When Jesus was tempted in the wilderness (Matthew 4:1–11), the devil tried to get him to act in ways that were incongruent with his true self, found only in God. For example, the devil tempted Jesus to turn some stones into bread, given that Jesus was extremely hungry. Also, the devil tried to get Jesus to jump off a temple so that angels could catch him. Finally, the devil attempted to get Jesus to worship the devil, promising he would give Jesus the "kingdoms of the world" if Jesus would just bow down to the devil. In each of these instances, Jesus stayed firmly connected to his true self, found exclusively in God, rather than relying on a false self that was overly concerned with what he accomplished, what other people thought of him, or what he possessed (Pennington, 2000). Therefore, whereas the false self is organized around what we accomplish, our reputation among others, and material possessions, the true self is hidden in God, relying on God from moment to moment.

In this exercise, please close your eyes, getting into a comfortable position. Place your feet on the floor, and sit up straight in a firm, supportive chair. In a quiet environment, simply sit in silence, watching your inner experiences from moment to moment. When you are ready, begin to notice a specific way you have relied on the false self over the years, defining your sense of self based on what you have accomplished, what other people have thought of you, or what you have owned in the form of material possessions. Spend about 20 minutes in silence, just noticing the thoughts and images that are connected to your false sense of self, without doing anything with them.

Now, when you are ready, imagine just letting go of the tendency to hold onto these thoughts and memories, similar to Jesus solely relying on God for nurturance and survival. Whenever a thought or memory arises related to what you do, what others think of you, or what you have, just envision letting go of the tendency to cling to this aspect of the false self. Just like Jesus stated that he would rely on God's word and worship God to get him through a difficult time, see if you can just rest in God's arms, rather than holding on to the false self.

When you are done with the 20-minute exercise, please write down some of your thoughts, memories, and feelings in the space that follows, identifying this aspect of the false self that you might be overly relying on in your life. Also, similar to Jesus relying on God's word, see if you can identify several key passages in scripture to meditate on when this part of the false self tends to arise from moment to moment, drawing from scripture to find your true self in God.

_____

_____

_____

_____

_____

_____

_____

Exercise: The Jesus Prayer

Given the emphasis in the *Philokalia* on developing the *nous* with the Jesus Prayer (see Smith, 2013), see if you can practice the prayer (consistent with prior chapters) over the course of the next 20 minutes. However, try to be especially mindful of the *mercy* you are asking for from Jesus. Because mercy signifies compassion *and* empathy, you are reaching out to God in a vulnerable state, asking him to literally reside inside of you, trusting that he knows you much more deeply than you know yourself (Talbot, 2013).

In fact, you are asking Jesus to offer you compassion, healing you as a physician who is caring for a patient in need of immediate assistance. Because God knows you more than you actually know yourself, you can let go of the verbal self, trusting you were made in his image. Certainly, you are a new creation in Christ—the old self is fully gone—based on Jesus' atonement on the cross (2 Corinthians 5:17).

As you say the prayer, "Lord Jesus Christ, Son of God, have mercy on me, a sinner," just acknowledge when your mind has wandered, reminiscent of noticing the verbal self in ACT, comprised of judgments, evaluations, and labels. Then, gently return to the prayer, attempting to experience God directly, beyond *dianoia* and the *logismoi* that tend to pull you away from an intuitive grasp of him. Again, trust in God, knowing that Jesus empathizes with your weaknesses (Hebrews 4:15), and takes up residence within your inner world. From an ACT perspective, you are detaching from your overreliance on the verbal self, offering the *logismoi* to him during this time.

Conclusion

In this chapter, you were able to learn about ACT's observing self, tapping into this sense of self to shift your perspective. Rather than employing the verbal self to make sense of inner and outer events, you were able to connect to the you that is watching your thoughts, feelings, and sensations, which can help you safely notice, with an open curiosity, rather than getting bullied around by changing intrapsychic experiences.

For desert Christians throughout the ages, the *nous* seems to similarly capture the *you* that is beyond words. In contrast to *dianoia*, as well as the *logismoi* that sometimes distract you from an awareness of God, the *nous* is your soul, which experiences God directly, transcending the limitations of language. Through the use of metaphors, exercises, and the Jesus Prayer, you were able to move in the direction of deepening your ability to reach out to God, letting go of an attachment to the verbal self.

In the next chapter, you will begin to explore values, which can offer a reliable, stable path for life. Rather than relying on fused thinking, distressing emotions, thoughts about the past or future, or a storied version of your self-concept, values are a way to head down a meaningful, impactful path from moment to moment. Therefore, ACT advocates for identifying with, and, more importantly, actively pursuing, predetermined principles that can guide the present moment.

For Christians, biblical virtues are much more specific than the general term, "values," and can help you to anchor your behavior to the Bible. Therefore, I review several biblical virtues, applying them to Jesus' life in order to help you follow him as the suffering servant and Messiah. To follow Jesus, you may continue to experience inner distress. Yet, by combining ACT's processes with contemplative Christianity, you may be better prepared to endure, trusting that God's providence is guiding the way.

Notes

1 Although a more formal discussion is beyond the scope of this workbook, it is important to note that, from a Christian perspective, the *nous* needs to be healed because of the fall of humankind (see, e.g., Mathewes-Green, 2009). On the other hand, with ACT, the observing self is stable, and does not need to change, given it is simply a viewpoint, perspective, or "pure awareness" (see, e.g., Harris, 2009).

2 The quotes in this section are from Smith (2013).

References

Amis, R. (1995). *A Different Christianity: Early Christian Esotericism and Modern Thought*. England: Praxis Institute Press.

Bangley, B. (Ed.) (2006). *The Cloud of Unknowing: Contemporary English Edition*. Brewster, MA: Paraclete Press.

Chumley, N. (2014). *Be Still and Know: God's Presence and Silence*. Minneapolis, MN: Augsburg Fortress.

Coniaris, A. (1998). *Philokalia: The Bible of Orthodox Spirituality*. Minneapolis, MN: Light & Life Publishing Company.

Coniaris, A. (2004). *Confronting and Controlling Thoughts According to the Fathers of the Philokalia*. Minneapolis, MN: Light & Life Publishing Co.

Harmless, W. (2004). *Desert Christians: An Introduction to the Literature of Early Monasticism*. New York: Oxford University Press.

Harris, R. (2009). *ACT Made Simple: An Easy-to-Read Primer on Acceptance and Commitment Therapy*. Oakland, CA: New Harbinger Publications, Inc.

Laird, M. (2006). *Into the Silent Land: A Guide to the Christian Practice of Contemplation*. New York: Oxford University Press.

Luoma, J., Hayes, S., & Walser, R. (2007). *Learning ACT: An Acceptance and Commitment Therapy Skills-Training Manual for Therapists*. Oakland, CA: New Harbinger Publications, Inc.

Mathewes-Green, F. (2009). *The Jesus Prayer: The Ancient Desert Prayer that Tunes the Heart of God*. Brewster, MA: Paraclete Press.

Nassif, B. (2012). *Bringing Jesus to the Desert: Uncover the Ancient Culture, Discover Hidden Meanings*. Grand Rapids, MI: Zondervan.

Segal, Z., Williams, M., & Teasdale, J. (2012). *Mindfulness-Based Cognitive Therapy for Depression* (2nd ed.). New York: The Guilford Press.

Smith, A. (2013). *Philokalia: The Eastern Christian Spiritual Texts*. Woodstock, VT: Skylight Paths Publishing.

Chapter 7: Values and Christian Virtues

Introduction

In this chapter, you will learn about ACT's values process, which can be helpful in providing a map for life. Rather than being guided by wavering thoughts and feelings, identifying and connecting to a set of distinct values can help you to press forward with consistency and commitment. Although difficult thoughts and feelings may seem especially persuasive, leading to fusion and avoidance, values can help you to engage with life again, doing what matters most in this short time you have to live the life God has planned for you.

As a Christian, you likely rely on the Bible to guide you on the paths of life. Within the Christian faith, identifying a set of biblical virtues (rather than the more general term, "values") can be helpful in directing your life as you walk behind Jesus. Therefore, in this chapter, you will learn about a variety of virtues that are rooted in the Christian tradition, drawing from early desert Christians' experiences, as well as virtues in the Bible. Given that following Jesus is central to Christian living, you will unpack a range of Jesus' teachings, which can offer a more specific, trustworthy trajectory for daily life.

Along the way, you will have the opportunity to prioritize a variety of biblical virtues, and explore ways to link virtuous living with your own life goals. As you move through this chapter, a special emphasis will be placed on the role that virtues play in helping you to walk behind Jesus, based on the notion that your thoughts and feelings likely have not provided a stable path from day to day. This shift, which is presented throughout the workbook, can help you accept your current pain so you can begin to live life again, "in the game" rather than "on the sidelines."

Since you are currently working on (a) relating to the *logismoi* with more distance and flexibility, (b) enduring painful emotions with a sense of hope, (c) staying in contact with God in each passing moment, and (d) connecting to the *nous,* identifying and committing to virtue-based action can offer you the paradigm shift you might be looking for. In other words, when you begin to surrender your inner world to God, trusting in his providence, you may find you are able to follow Jesus more confidently, committing to biblical virtues that will illuminate the future paths he has called you to walk with him on.

ACT's Values Process

Within ACT, values are defined as "chosen life directions," and have the following characteristics (Harris, 2009; Hayes, Strosahl, & Wilson, 2012):

- Values are continuous, rather than changing from minute to minute.
- Values offer a "bigger picture" perspective, instead of being disorganized or fragmented.
- Values are anchored to the present moment, rather than found in the past or future.
- Values are chosen freely, based on what matters most, instead of being adopted solely because of parental or societal expectations.
- Values are intimately linked to concrete, behavioral action, rather than embraced abstractly.

Ultimately, values unfold in the here and now, are based on what matters deeply, lead to effective action, and tend to be "verbs" rather than "nouns" (Stoddard & Afari, 2014).

To offer a quick example, suppose you want to be a loving spouse. From a values perspective, loving is continuous, offering a "bigger picture" perspective. In addition, being loving is something you can *be* in the here and now, choosing freely to engage in loving behavior as you interact with your partner today. Finally, because you value being a loving spouse, you inevitably choose to *act* on this value, rather than merely thinking about being loving in your mind.

From an ACT perspective, values are especially salient because they can help you to head down a stable path, intentionally creating a life that matters to you. On the other hand, when you do not have a set of values to help you decide which direction to take, you may find that you are frequently bullied around by your mind, choosing the way to go based on what your mind tells you. In addition, you might discover that you are deciding on certain paths based on what will lead to the least amount of psychological pain, avoiding the trails of life that are most important to you simply because they involve some degree of distress.

Because values tend to be global principles (Harris, 2009), there are a plethora of common values that may look familiar to you; still, you might have lost your connection to them, based in part on fusion and avoidance. In either case, below are some values that you may find helpful in order to begin the brainstorming process (adapted from Harris, 2013):

- Compassionate
- Creative
- Dependable
- Forgiving
- Genuine
- Healthy
- Humble
- Kind
- Loving
- Trusting

As this list reveals, there are a wide variety of values that you can connect to from moment to moment to guide your life. Many of these values, to be sure, can send you in a different direction than your thoughts and feelings, which fluctuate and change as you cross days off the calendar of life. When you overly rely on your mind, you may quickly approach the "fork in the road" (Hayes, 2005) mentioned in a prior chapter. At this point, you can choose to head in either a valued direction (which may involve some pain) or down the road of a seemingly pain-free life (which can also result in added pain, though, given that you are "playing it safe").

Within the ACT literature, the "compass metaphor" (see, e.g., Harris, 2009; Hayes et al., 2012) is often used to capture the values process. Similar to a compass, values are a direction you head in life, rather than a goal, which can be crossed off a "to do" list. Consistent with heading "west" or "east," you can wake up in the morning and head in the direction of being "loving" or "kind." On the other hand, a goal is something that has an end point, as in the distinction between pursuing learning (a value) and signing up for a community college class (a goal). Notice, though, that values need to be linked to goals in order to live them out in a concrete manner.

In the space that follows, see if you can identify some of your own values (rather than goals), which you might have lost sight of over the years based on your current struggles with an emotional disorder.

1 _____

2 _____

3 _____

4 _____

5 _____

Within the ACT model, however, values are not synonymous with morals, given that morals are linked to behavior deemed "right" or "wrong" in a particular society, culture, or religious system (Harris, 2009). Therefore, because values are personally chosen, they are not inherently consistent (although they might be) with the Christian tradition. Since virtues, by contrast, are about moral principles—"right" and "wrong" behavior—you may want to further explore some of the Christian virtues that have been identified and lived out over the last two millennia.

Worded differently, the Christian faith has a variety of virtues that can guide life, too. Many of these virtues, certainly, seem to overlap with ACT's values process. Therefore, what follows is a review of early desert Christians' desire to live out a wide variety of virtues, emulating Jesus Christ as they humbly learned to live in community with one another. Following this discussion, I review virtues in the Bible, Martha's servanthood, and Jesus' teachings, all in an effort to help you develop a list of well-defined virtues to live life, following Jesus with a sense of hope and commitment.

Early Desert Christians and Virtues
Among the early desert Christians, virtuous living was a central aim. In fact, because monks in the harsh desert terrain struggled in their cell with a variety of tempting, compulsive thoughts, they turned to virtue-based action as a way to combat the *logismoi*. As they cultivated the ability to ameliorate the grip that the inner world had on them, they were able to organically turn towards virtues as a way to guide life (Harmless, 2008). In other words, through the regular

practice of wordless, imageless prayer, desert monks learned to gently observe the inner world with a detached watchfulness and inner calm. The 4th-century monk Evagrius Ponticus called this process "passionlessness" (Harmless, 2008).

Reminiscent of ACT's proposed shift from relying on fused thoughts and the avoidance of emotions to values to determine a course of action, early desert Christians developed the ability to notice the *logismoi* in the cell with patience, endurance, and vigilant watchfulness, pivoting towards a variety of biblical virtues to guide life, characteristic of Jesus. Some of the virtues they embodied included chastity, self-control, love, persistence, forgiveness, kindness, and humility (see Jamison, 2008), which are frequently referred to as the *seven virtues*.

Below are some behavioral examples of 21st-century individuals living out the seven virtues, in spite of ongoing pain emanating from an emotional disorder:

- Mike historically struggled with viewing pornography, turning to the Internet to numb his pain, especially when he was experiencing social anxiety; yet, over time, he was able to learn to let his anxiety run its natural course, enduring the pain in order to pursue the virtue of chastity. As a result, he made the decision to deepen his relationship with his wife via virtue-based action.
- Aaron used to turn to overeating as a way to seemingly manage his depression, avoiding low mood by attempting to distract himself from depressive symptoms; still, in psychotherapy, he learned to shift to the Mary mode, simply resting at Jesus' feet. In turn, he pivoted towards living out the virtue of self-control, letting go of the tendency to reach for food when he felt down.
- For Heidi, daily worry seemed inevitable, leading to trouble sleeping and impaired functioning at work. However, she slowly learned how to focus on God's presence, letting go of the tendency to want to predict her future with a sense of certainty. Rather, she allowed her worry to arise and pass away, shifting towards loving children in the youth ministry at her church, practicing the virtue of charity.
- As a child, Peter was repeatedly neglected by his father, leading to an adulthood filled with loneliness, intense sadness, and recurrent panic attacks that seemed to come out of nowhere. During especially difficult weeks, Peter would isolate himself, staying

indoors in fear of another panic attack. When at home, he would frequently dwell on his apparent "worthlessness," struggling to understand how his father could just leave him at such a young age. Increasingly, though, Peter learned to accept his inner experiences with endurance, based on the hope that Jesus would eventually restore all things. He also began to pursue the virtue of forgiveness, recognizing that he could forgive his father because of Jesus' model of self-emptying service.

- When Jennifer started experiencing social anxiety as a young adult, her weeks seemed to go on forever, given that she had to interact frequently with people at work. When she felt especially anxious, she would call in sick, doubting that she could truly do her best in an anxious state. Yet, she started to work on defusing from some of her thoughts about being rejected by others, allowing her thinking to run its natural course, consistent with early desert Christians' response to the *logismoi* in the cell. Over time, as she made room for these inner experiences, given that Jesus was with her, she was able to focus on the virtue of kindness, responding to customers like she believed Jesus would.

- In his daily life, Juan repeatedly worried from one topic to the next, struggling to accept the ambiguity of an unknown future. When he felt especially anxious, he would try to control his world through compulsively checking his work and searching the Internet for answers to a variety of questions. As Juan began to learn how to just notice these thoughts, without reacting to them, he was able to cultivate the virtue of humility, using the Jesus Prayer to ask Jesus for healing from moment to moment. As he cried out to God, he found that he could increasingly let go of his need to control, humbly sitting at Jesus' feet in order to surrender to God's providential care.

As these examples reveal, faith-based ACT is about learning to be watchful with the inner world, deepening your ability to endure painful inner experiences with a sense of hope and patience. Because God is present, your most difficult inner experiences can be surrendered to him, trusting that he has only the best of intentions for you. In that you are focused less on getting rid of the inner word, recognizing that not all of your compulsive, tempting thoughts are "true," you can pivot towards following Jesus, devoting your time and energy to living out a variety of specific virtues, reminiscent of early desert Christians.

Below are several teachings from the *Sayings of the Desert Fathers*[1] that capture their dedication to cultivating virtuous behavior, reminiscent of Jesus Christ:

- "One of the fathers used to say that a person ought before all things to acquire belief in God, a ceaseless yearning for God, guilelessness, not returning evil for evil, mortification and humility, purity, clemency and love for all, submission, gentleness, long-suffering, patience, a desire for God, and [the practice of] constantly calling upon God with a painful heart and genuine love, with a view to not paying attention to what is past but attending to that which is to come, having no confidence in one's own good works and service, and ceaselessly invoking the help of God in the things that happen to one each day."
- "Let us practice gentleness and long-suffering, forbearance, and love, for in these the monk consists."
- "Before all else, the monk ought to practice humble-mindedness, for it is the first commandment of the Savior, saying, 'Blessed are the poor in spirit, for theirs is the kingdom of heaven.'"
- "A person is as much in need of humble-mindedness all the time and of the fear of God as he is of the breath that comes out of his mouth."
- "Do your utmost to do nobody any harm whatsoever; keep your heart pure with everybody."
- "Love is conversation with God in unbroken thanksgiving, for God rejoices in thanksgiving; it is an indication of repose."

As these sayings reveal, the early desert Christians were especially focused on humility and love, among other virtues. What is more, one of the most important virtues was detachment, given that they spent a great deal of time facing the inner world with an attitude of watchfulness and endurance.

Exercise: Detachment as a Central Desert Virtue
For early desert Christians, moving to the desert was just as much about a spiritual attitude of detachment and "freedom from care" as it was about letting go of their actual material possessions (Burton-Christie, 1993). This outer freedom ended up deepening an inner freedom, leading to the ability to trust in God's providential care from moment to moment, rather than a false sense of security and safety. Drawing from Jesus' Sermon on the Mount, desert monks strived to

let go of worry, recognizing that God would provide for them, reminiscent of his loving care for the birds and flowers (Matthew 6:25–34):

- "Therefore I tell you, do not worry about your life, what you will eat or drink; or about your body, what you will wear. Is not life more than food, and the body more than clothes? Look at the birds of the air; they do not sow or reap or store away in barns, and yet your heavenly Father feeds them. Are you not much more valuable than they? Can any one of you by worrying add a single hour to your life? And why do you worry about clothes? See how the flowers of the field grow. They do not labor or spin. Yet I tell you that not even Solomon in all his splendor was dressed like one of these. If that is how God clothes the grass of the field, which is here today and tomorrow is thrown into the fire, will he not much more clothe you—you of little faith? So do not worry, saying, 'What shall we eat?' or 'What shall we drink?' or 'What shall we wear?' For the pagans run after all these things, and your heavenly Father knows that you need them. But seek first his kingdom and his righteousness, and all these things will be given to you as well. Therefore do not worry about tomorrow, for tomorrow will worry about itself. Each day has enough trouble of its own."

If possible, try to imagine what your life might be like if you were able to let go of a preoccupation with worry, allowing these types of thoughts to simply pass on by, without trying to clutch them or drive them away. Instead, what might it be like to fully trust in God's providence, consistent with Jesus' teaching in Matthew? Worded differently, similar to the early desert Christians, how might your life be different if you were able to move in the direction of embracing a spiritual attitude of detachment in daily living, letting go of a preoccupation with both the inner and outer world and trusting that God will intervene?

If you can, try to reflect on this type of a life in the space below, considering the following questions:

- What might it be like to detach from your most distressing thoughts and feelings, trusting that God is sovereign over your inner world?
- How might life be different if you let go of the tendency to hold onto your own inner efforts to control, predict, and attain absolute certainty about life?

- What possessions in the outer world might you need to let go of, given that you may be distracted, in order to shift your focus towards God instead?
- With this newly found freedom within the inner world, letting go of attachments and worry, how might you be able to follow Jesus more authentically?
- Which virtues can you focus on living out, based on this newly acquired ability to relinquish the tight grip—that is, an attitude of possessiveness—you have on the inner and outer world?

_____

_____

_____

_____

_____

_____

_____

_____

The Freedom to Choose Virtues

Within the ACT model, values are freely chosen from person to person (Hayes, 2005). In other words, values, which are "chosen life directions" (Hayes, 2005), are not to be pushed on you in any way. Although there are often lists of common values available in the ACT literature, these examples merely serve as a starting point, rather than some sort of requirement for value-based action. Therefore, it is important to remember that you are free to choose your own values, rather than fusing with someone else's list of what your life should look like. When it comes to creating a meaningful, vibrant life, you are the cartographer, and you get to draw the map.

As a Christian, though, Jesus has invited you to follow _him_ (Matthew 4:19), reminiscent of his offer to the disciples in the gospels. As a result of this invitation, each disciple had a personal decision to make, divorced from coercion, power, or manipulation. Although a dozen disciples responded to the call, dropping what they were doing to follow Jesus, some accounts in the gospels involved individuals declining Jesus' invite (see, e.g., Mark 10). Thus, following Jesus each day (rooted in moral behavior) needs to be a personal decision on your part, rather than something forced onto you by parents, society, or a well-intentioned religious institution.

To be more specific, virtuous living is about a *relationship* with Jesus, becoming more like him each day, rather than a list of moral behaviors that you *must* follow. After all, Jesus consistently seemed to highlight that the Pharisees were too focused on moral behavior, noting they appeared to be hypocrites in daily life. In one account, certainly, Jesus described the Pharisees as "whitewashed tombs" (Matthew 23:27).

As you continue on with the workbook, try to remember that virtues naturally emanate from an authentic relationship with Jesus, reminiscent of wanting to be a better spouse, rooted in love, rather than coercion, guilt, or fear. This theme will be explored a bit more in a subsequent section of this chapter. For now, though, see if you can begin to identify key virtues found in the pages of the Bible.

Virtues in the Bible

In the New Testament, three theological virtues are mentioned, including faith, hope, and love (see, e.g., 1 Corinthians 13:13). As a guide for life, *faith* can be especially important when you do not know what lies ahead, yielding to God's providence from moment to moment. Moreover, *hope* can allow you to recognize that God will eventually restore all things. This understanding of the future can be especially important when you are currently struggling with an emotional disorder, enduring difficult inner experiences in order to press on, following Jesus as he guides you through life. Finally, *love* is a central virtue within the Christian life, reflecting Jesus' atoning work on the cross (see, e.g., John 3:16).

Still, as you pursue virtue-based living, attempting to follow Jesus where he would have you go, you will come up short. In fact, you might find yourself wandering off the path God has called you to walk with him on, "missing the mark." When this happens, having a set of virtues to guide your behavior can be especially salient, given that God's word is a light for your path (Psalm 119:105). Certainly, because Jesus offers grace and mercy, empathizing with your struggles, you can approach his "throne of grace" with confidence (see Hebrews 4), quickly getting back on the road again to follow him.

Virtues and the Martha Mode

In the story of Mary and Martha in the gospel of Luke, Mary patiently sat at the feet of Jesus, consistent with the "being" mode mentioned in prior chapters; on the other hand, Martha served Jesus, reminiscent of the "doing" mode (Williams, 2008). Although Jesus ultimately preferred Mary's behavior, Martha exemplified an attitude of servanthood and self-sacrifice, something that Jesus repeatedly taught about and advocated for (see, e.g., Matthew 20:28). Because of this, the Christian life involves both "being," resting at the feet of Jesus to learn from him and surrender to his will, and "doing," actively following him and serving in love.

Above all else, the Mary and Martha distinction can help to illuminate the importance of *both* contemplation *and* action, balancing the two in order to yield to God's will for your life. In fact, it may be helpful for you to view Mary's submissive posture as capturing the inner world, letting go of the tendency to fix or problem solve, just trusting that Jesus is active and present. Shedding your efforts to control your thoughts and feelings, certainly, can help you to pivot towards focusing on Jesus as you patiently surrender to his providential care.

Yet, when it comes to the outer world, an attitude of servanthood and self-sacrifice can help you to walk passionately behind Jesus, striving to be like him in his ability to respond to those in need. As your rabbi, suffering servant, and Messiah, Jesus can help you to cultivate virtue-based action, recognizing when to sit at his feet and when to follow him through the door and out into the world to make a change for the better, putting his kingdom first. The "wisdom to know the difference" is especially important, as Reinhold Niebuhr's *Serenity Prayer* suggests:

- "God grant me the serenity to accept the things I cannot change; courage to change the things I can; and wisdom to know the difference. Living one day at a time; enjoying one moment at a time; accepting hardships as the pathway to peace; taking, as He did, this sinful world as it is, not as I would have it; trusting that He will make all things right if I surrender to His Will; that I may be reasonably happy in this life and supremely happy with Him forever in the next. Amen."

The Teachings of Jesus as a Guide for Life

In Jesus' Sermon on the Mount (see Matthew 5–7), he revealed several biblical virtues for Christians to live by. To begin, he mentioned that the "poor in spirit" are "blessed," consistent with early desert

Christians' emphasis on emulating Jesus' humility and "self empty-ing" (Burton-Christie, 1993). To be sure, as noted above, detachment was not just about letting go of material possessions, as in "blessed are the poor." Rather, to be "poor in spirit" was about fully surrender-ing the inner world to God, too.

Further along in the Sermon on the Mount, Jesus taught about the importance of forgiveness, love, non-judgment, and letting go of worry, consistent with the early desert Christians' teachings. Each of these teachings, for desert monks, was foundational in their walk with Jesus, attempting to be like him as they surrendered to God's will in the hot desert landscape. Although you most likely do not live in the wilderness, you may find that Jesus' teachings are just as rel-evant today as they were some 1,700 years ago for monks living in the deserts of Egypt and Syria. In fact, for devoted Christians, follow-ing Jesus is just as important now as it was back then.

Virtues, the Teachings of Jesus, and Emotional Disorders

To relate Jesus' teachings to emotional disorders, thus far, you have learned about a variety of strategies to (a) watch your think-ing patterns with a bit more distance; (b) accept and endure pain-ful emotions with a sense of hope, patience, and perseverance; (c) connect to God in each and every moment, surrendering to his will; and (d) experience God directly, beyond distracting thoughts and feelings. Because you have worked towards relating to the inner world with a bit more tentativeness, your thoughts and feelings are less likely to bully you around as you walk through life. Instead, as you deepen your awareness of God's active, loving presence, you may find you are more aware of his plan for you.

To relate to your depressive or anxiety-related symptoms with more open curiosity (and less rigidity) means you are inviting God into your inner world, trusting that he is in control. Therefore, instead of looking to wavering thoughts and feelings, which tend to fluctuate and change from day to day, you can begin to turn to Jesus' teach-ings to guide your life. After all, Jesus confidently said the following (Matthew 7:24–27):

- "Therefore everyone who hears these words of mine and puts them into practice is like a wise man who built his house on the rock. The rain came down, the streams rose, and the winds blew and beat against that house; yet it did not fall, because it had its foundation on the rock. But everyone who hears these words of mine and does not put them into practice is like a foolish man who built his house on sand. The rain came down, the streams rose, and the winds blew and beat against that house, and it fell with a great crash."

Exercise: The Wise Builder

In this exercise, I would like for you to imagine you are the "wise builder" that Jesus mentioned at the end of the Sermon on the Mount. As Jesus revealed, this wise person built a house on solid rock, which represents radically living out Jesus' teachings. Moreover, try to imagine that your current psychiatric symptoms represent the "rain," "streams," and "wind" in Jesus' account of the "wise builder." Here you are, with your house firmly fastened to a stable foundation.

As the storm approaches, consisting of difficult thoughts, feelings, and sensations, you are able to pivot towards virtue-based action, living out Jesus' teachings. Worded differently, even though the storm comes, with additional storms on the way, you are able to apply Jesus' divine plan to your life, forgiving others, practicing non-judgment, letting go of worry, praying for others, and serving those in need.

If you can, try to begin to think about some concrete ways you can live out Jesus' teachings in the Sermon on the Mount, even though the storms of life (i.e., depressive or anxiety-related symptoms) continue to come. In other words, what might you actually *do*—in behavioral terms—to put Jesus' words into practice, rather than just hearing them and walking away? How might your life be different if you were applying Jesus' teachings in each and every moment, rather than just knowing about them abstractly, reminiscent of a house built on sand?

Virtues Metaphors

Given that ACT frequently uses metaphors to help you better understand its six core processes, what follows are a variety of metaphors to help you better live out your virtues, letting the inner world continue to do what it will do, following Jesus in spite of psychological pain:

- Virtue-based living is like building my house on the rock (Matthew 7:24–27). I can let the storms of the inner world just pass on by, without letting the bad weather determine what I am going to do, given that Jesus' teachings are my guide for life.

- Virtue-based living is like continuously heading home to Jesus, especially when I notice I have wandered away, consistent with the Parable of the Lost Son (Luke 15:11–32). I can just accept my inner world, knowing that God is welcoming me home with loving arms. The most important part of my journey is heading in the right direction, even when I have wandered away because I have fused with distressing thoughts or avoided painful feelings.
- Virtue-based living is like following Jesus, as one of his disciples, even though some of my fellow disciples might be difficult to live with. Similarly, I can live out Jesus' teachings even though my thoughts and feelings might sometimes be painful.
- Virtue-based living is like Peter confidently walking to Jesus on the lake (see Matthew 14:22–23). At times, I might feel like I am sinking, fusing with thoughts of doubt and feelings of anxiety. Still, Jesus is with me, and can help me to continue to walk towards him, following his teachings along the way.[2]
- Just like Peter, I can continue to follow Jesus when I make a mistake, even after I have wandered away from him. Although Peter denied Jesus three times in the gospels (see, e.g., Luke 22), he went on to be a foundational figure in the 1st-century church. Similarly, although I might wander away from God's path due to fusion and avoidance, I can quickly get back on track, given that Jesus offers me grace and mercy in my walk with him.[3]

In these metaphors, notice that the central theme is continuing to walk with Jesus, even when your inner world can be difficult, overwhelming, or confusing. Although you may find that you have wandered away from time to time, the most important part of your journey with Jesus is to quickly get back on the path when you have drifted or straggled away. In other words, with virtues, try to think of them in behavioral terms, reminiscent of literally following Jesus, rather than in an abstract manner. Consistent with ACT, living a meaningful, deeply fulfilling life involves taking action, rather than "playing it safe."

Exercise: Starting the Journey

In Luke's gospel, Jesus instructed his disciples to head out on their journey in order to heal those who were sick, preaching "the kingdom of God" (see, e.g., Luke 9). On the journey, they were to leave behind all of their possessions, including food and money. As they pressed forward, they were to rely on God's providence, trusting that he would provide for them as they went from town to town (Green, 1997).

To draw a parallel, following Jesus will inevitably involve leaving some things behind, given that you are focused on trusting him on the roads of life. Stated differently, putting your faith in God requires letting go of control as you travel from town to town. In this exercise, see if you can identify some of the inner experiences you need to let go of as you pivot towards virtue-based action.

Rather than letting go of food and clothing, are there certain thoughts that you have historically been fused with? How about distressing emotions that have determined the direction you have headed in? With this exercise, see if you can "leave behind" (i.e., let go of the tendency to overly rely on, rather than try to permanently get rid of) certain thoughts and feelings as you head out on your journey with Jesus.

Thoughts I will let go of as I follow Jesus, engaging in virtue-based action:

_____

_____

_____

_____

_____

_____

_____

_____

_____

Feelings I will accept as I follow Jesus, engaging in virtue-based action:

_____

_____

_____

_____

Exercise: Identifying Christian Virtues in the Bible

In the space that follows, I would like for you to continue to develop an awareness of biblical virtues that can guide your life as you follow Jesus from moment to moment. Therefore, see if you can identify key passages in the Bible that reveal virtuous living. If you can, try to identify the biblical characters involved and how they demonstrated moral behavior. Also, try to discuss the end result, if there is an end to the story. Finally, try to consider the lesson learned, and God's view of the behavior, if it is available in the text.

_____

_____

_____

_____

_____

_____

_____

_____

_____

Exercise: My Favorite Character in the Bible[4]

For this exercise, see if you can identify your favorite character in the Bible. Maybe this is an Old Testament story that you grew up with, recalling that your mother or father told you this story when you were very young. Or, this might be a biblical character that has especially influenced you over the years. In either case, go to the place in the Bible that describes the character, and see if you can identify some of the virtues that the character lived by. In other words, what did he or she stand for, and how did he or she create a meaningful life, pleasing God in the process?

Now, see if you can apply some of these virtues to your own life. How, in the 21st century, can you also please God, reminiscent of this esteemed character? How can you go about doing so from moment to moment as you strive to live a life filled with moral behavior, rooted in scripture? What obstacles might get in your way, and how can you overcome the obstacles, consistent with your chosen character? When you are finished, see if you can jot down some of the answers to the aforementioned questions.

_____

_____

_____

_____

_____

_____

_____

_____

Exercise: Jesus' Teachings from the Sermon on the Mount

In addition to the above exercise, see if you can identify specific teachings from Jesus' Sermon on the Mount that you would like to start living by today, in this moment. Try to be as specific as you can, imagining that you are literally following Jesus as you embody the various teachings you have selected.

1 _____

2 _____

3 _____

4 _____

5 _____

6 _____

7 _____

8 _____

9 _____

10 _____

Exercise: Standing Before God

In this exercise, I would like for you to imagine that you have lived a long life. Standing before God, you are ready to receive feedback directly from God about how you lived your days on Earth. In this time spent with him, what would you like for him to say? In other words, how would you like him to describe your life, in behavioral terms? How would you like for him to depict your walk with Jesus? What types of virtues would you like for him to highlight, which are pleasing to him and capture your heart for God? In the space that follows, see if you can write down some biblical virtues that you would like God to mention, describing in detail what you would like for him to observe in your daily life?

1 _____

2 _____

3 _____

4 _____

5 _____

Exercise: Christian Virtues in Major Life Areas

In the last few exercises, you have had the opportunity to identify and apply several biblical virtues to your life. Now, see if you can apply these virtues across a variety of major life arenas. Stated differently, how would you like to demonstrate these moral behaviors in several areas of your life? If you can, try to be concise in your descriptions, reflecting on how you would like to embody the virtues as actions in purely behavioral terms.

Family life: _____

_____

Marital life: _____

_____

Work life: _____

_____

Church life: _____

_____

Spiritual life: _____

_____

Community life: _____

_____

Exercise: Connecting to the Process of Following Jesus

ACT has a famous saying: "Outcome is the process through which process can become the outcome" (Hayes, Strosahl, & Wilson, 1999, p. 221). Although somewhat confusing, the phrase means that living life by pursuing values is a lifelong journey. In fact, value-based action is both the means and the end, whereas focusing exclusively on goals can result in chasing the carrot, just out of reach, which is dangling from the proverbial stick. In other words, goals are down the road, rather than a process unfolding in the present moment. Because of this, when you are solely focused on goals, life can be filled with discontentment, given that there is constantly a discrepancy between where you are and where you want to be. Certainly, this "gap" can lead to a "coming up short" experience.

Similarly, in the Christian life, focusing only on goals—especially when they are wrapped up solely in moral behavior, emphasizing some sort of list of demands about how you should function—can leave you feeling discouraged. There is always some other state or trait to be achieved, divorced from a more intimate union with God. On the other hand, by focusing on following Jesus, receiving his grace and mercy along the way, you are beginning a lifelong journey of cultivating a deeper awareness of God's active, loving presence, attending to the relationship at hand, with virtuous behavior organically emanating from your trust in him. Worded differently, virtuous living is a byproduct of trusting in Jesus, rather than a foundational goal.

In the space that follows, please reflect on your current relationship with Jesus in order to focus on Jesus as the source of life (John 14:6). Since I will be asking you in a subsequent section to establish several goals, it can be helpful to first remind yourself that goals naturally flow from virtues, which are rooted in a relationship with Jesus Christ. To draw a parallel with nature, snow gently falls on top of a mountain, which melts away, turning into water and flowing down a river bed; this melted snow eventually forms a waterfall, which pools into a small pond at the foot of the mountain. In this process, the water in the pond can eventually be traced back to the source.

In the below section, see if you can explore ways to deepen your relationship with Jesus, based on some of the suggestions previously outlined in this workbook, as well as what types of virtues might organically flow from this intimate union, assuming you are able to move in the direction of surrendering to Jesus in an authentic, passionate way.

_____

_____

_____

_____

_____

_____

_____

_____

Exercise: Linking Virtues to Goals

In order to live out your identified virtues, following Jesus along the way as you build a relationship with him, see if you can formulate some concrete goals, rooted in scripture, linking them to virtues found in the Bible. In other words, try to develop a plan of action, listing out several key virtues, the goals you will abide by to carry them out, and the passages in scripture that support the virtues/goals as moral behavior.

With goals, they need to be measurable, attainable, positive, and specific (*MAPS*; Chang, Scott, & Decker, 2013). To be measurable, goals need to be quantifiable (e.g., "I will run three times this week because I value physical health"). Moreover, goals need to be attainable, meaning you can actually achieve them. Training to run a marathon next week (with no prior running experience) is an unreasonable target, whereas working towards running a half-marathon in six months is more feasible. In addition, goals need to be positive in how you describe them, emphasizing something you *will* do, rather than *will not* do (e.g., "I will volunteer in a church ministry because I value serving others" versus "I will not socially isolate myself this week"). Finally, goals need to be as concrete and specific as possible, rather than vague or overly general (e.g., "I will go to dinner and the movies with my spouse this week" versus "I will spend more time with my spouse"). The more specific you can be, the better you will be able to head in the direction of your goals, monitoring how well you are doing in achieving them.

In the box below, see if you can list out several virtues, linking them to both goals that are *MAPS* and passages in scripture.

Virtue			
	Goal		
		Scripture to Support the Virtue/Goal	

(*Continued*)

Virtue			
	Goal		
		Scripture to Support the Virtue/Goal	
Virtue			
	Goal		
		Scripture to Support the Virtue/Goal	
Virtue			
	Goal		
		Scripture to Support the Virtue/Goal	

Conclusion

In this chapter, you reviewed ACT's values process, learning about the role that value-based living plays in creating a meaningful life. Instead of being guided by wavering thoughts and feelings, values can help to offer a stable "compass" (Hayes, 2005), allowing you to head in a valued direction from moment to moment. On the roads of life, you will most certainly find that you have drifted from time to time. When this happens, values can serve as a map to get you back on your chosen path, allowing your thoughts and feelings to come along for the ride, even when they are difficult and unrelenting.

For early desert Christians, virtues were especially salient, helping them to follow Jesus in the harsh desert terrain. Among other examples of moral behavior, humility, love, and detachment allowed them to emulate Jesus, self-emptying in order to surrender to God's providential care. In your own life, you may find that it is especially powerful to identify and commit to a set of virtues to guide your paths, locating examples of moral behavior within the pages of the Bible.

Yet, virtuous living is much more than a set of behaviors to guide life. Jesus has invited you to walk with him, deepening your trust in him as you surrender to his plan. This path, though, involves a choice on your part, and is in no way coercive. Still, as you follow him, virtues can help you to better understand the map that embodies Jesus' life of servanthood and self-sacrifice.

In the next chapter, you will explore willingness and committed action, which is the thrust behind virtues. In order to live them out, courage is required, given that merely knowing *about* virtues does not necessary lead to action, becoming more like Jesus in daily living. As you begin to conclude this workbook, willingness can help you to shift from an abstract to concrete understanding of virtues, actually walking with Jesus on the path he has called you to travel with him on.

Notes

1 The sayings in this section are quoted from Wortley (2012). Used with permission.
2 This metaphor is influenced by Wilson and DuFrene's (2010) example of Peter's struggle to live out his faith in the gospel accounts.
3 This metaphor is influenced by Wilson and DuFrene's (2010) example of Peter's struggle to live out his faith in the gospel accounts.
4 This exercise is a modified version of a similar activity in Stoddard and Afari (2014).

References

Burton-Christie, D. (1993). *The Word in the Desert: Scripture and the Quest for Holiness in Early Christian Monasticism.* New York: Oxford University Press.

Chang, V., Scott, S., & Decker, C. (2013). *Developing Helping Skills: A Step-by-Step Approach to Competency* (2nd ed.). Belmont, CA: Brooks/Cole.

Green, J. (1997). *The Gospel of Luke.* Grand Rapids, MI: Wm. B. Eerdmans Publishing Co.

Harmless, W. (2008). *Mystics.* New York: Oxford University Press.

Harris, R. (2009). *ACT Made Simple: An Easy-to-Read Primer on Acceptance and Commitment Therapy.* Oakland, CA: New Harbinger Publications, Inc.

Harris, R. (2013). *Getting Unstuck with ACT: A Clinician's Guide to Overcoming Common Obstacles to Acceptance and Commitment Therapy.* Oakland, CA: New Harbinger Publications, Inc.

Hayes, S. (2005). *Get Out of Your Mind and Into Your Life: The New Acceptance & Commitment Therapy.* Oakland, CA: New Harbinger Publications, Inc.

Hayes, S., Strosahl, K., & Wilson, K. (1999). *Acceptance and Commitment Therapy: An Experiential Approach to Behavior Change.* New York: The Guilford Press.

Hayes, S., Strosahl, K., & Wilson, K. (2012). *Acceptance and Commitment Therapy: The Process and Practice of Mindful Change* (2nd ed.). New York: The Guilford Press.

Jamison, C. (2008). *Finding Happiness: Monastic Steps for a Fulfilling Life.* Collegeville, MN: Liturgical Press.

Stoddard, J., & Afari, N. (2014). *The Big Book of ACT Metaphors: A Practitioner's Guide to Experiential Exercises & Metaphors in Acceptance & Commitment Therapy.* Oakland, CA: New Harbinger Publications, Inc.

Williams, M. (2008). Mindfulness, depression and modes of mind. *Cognitive Therapy Research, 32,* 721–733.

Wilson, K., & DuFrene, T. (2010). *Things Might Go Terribly, Horribly Wrong: A Guide to Life Liberated from Anxiety.* Oakland, CA: New Harbinger Publications, Inc.

Wortley, J. (2012). *The Book of Elders: Sayings of the Desert Fathers.* Trappist, KY: Cistercian Publications.

Chapter 8: Committed Action and Following Jesus

Introduction

In this chapter, you will explore ACT's committed action process, which can help you to live out your values, rather than merely ponder them in an abstract manner. To actually "put the car in drive," placing one foot in front of the other to get into the swing of life again, requires a willingness to press forward, in spite of what your mind says about any perceived obstacles that are in the way. Willingness, therefore, is about having the courage to create the type of life you can be proud of, even though you may continue to experience psychological pain in the process.

Within the Christian faith, Jesus most certainly modeled a courageous willingness to push on, even as he walked with his cross to be executed. Therefore, as a Christian, you have the gospel accounts of Jesus' life, death, and resurrection, as well as a real relationship with him, to help you better understand the importance of enduring, even when life is unrelenting and painful. As someone who lived a perfect life (2 Corinthians 5:21), drawing you into a relationship with him (Luke 15:1–7), Jesus paved the way for virtue-based action, capturing optimal living during his brief stint in this world.

For the early desert Christians, life was also about taking action, especially as they said goodbye to the ways of the world, choosing to let go of all the distractions that got in the way of a deeper union with God. Turning to the desert, these Christian monks sought to fully trust in God's providence, demonstrating a commitment to their Lord and Savior that involved behavioral action. Rather than merely talking about following Jesus, they believed that the best way to do so was to let go of their possessions to walk radically behind Jesus, facing their temptations as they learned to accept the harsh, unforgiving desert landscape.

To be committed to Christian virtues, thus, means fully engaging with life, quite literally walking with Jesus where he would have you go. Similar to Jesus' disciples, who each made a very personal decision to follow him for several years before launching their own ministries, you are tasked with determining whether or not to surrender to God's plan, which can offer you the opportunity to transcend the current patterns that are keeping you stuck. In this chapter, you will integrate all six ACT processes to faithfully and authentically follow Jesus, your rabbi, suffering servant, and Messiah.

ACT's Committed Action Process

In the last chapter, you explored ACT's values process (Hayes, Strosahl, & Wilson, 2012), which involves connecting to a set of meaningful principles that can guide your life. Chosen freely and without coercion, values are rooted in the present moment, offering you a "big picture" perspective so that you have a trustworthy flashlight to illuminate your paths. More than anything else, values are synonymous with action, given that one cannot exist without the other. Because values are heartfelt, offering you an opportunity to connect to what matters most in this world, they tend to be much more consistent than wavering thoughts and feelings, which may change from day to day and minute to minute.

To understand committed action (Hayes et al., 2012), it is important to integrate all six of ACT's processes, given that ACT is really about purposeful behavior. In other words, foundationally, ACT is an approach that emphasizes living the life you want, without getting tossed to and fro on the seas of life, shipwrecked by the storms of the inner world. Therefore, the below *FEAR* (capturing the problem) and *ACT* (offering the solution) acronyms (adapted from Hayes et al., 2012) can be helpful in combining the ACT puzzle pieces together to form a coherent picture:

- *F* = Fusing with difficult thoughts, automatically assuming they are "true" and "accurate."
- *E* = Evaluating and judging inner experiences, especially painful thoughts, feelings, and sensations.
- *A* = Avoiding both inner and outer experiences, leading to feeling stuck on the sidelines of life.
- *R* = Reason giving, offering clever, "valid" excuses for why now is not the right time to live a life that is consistent with your values.

- *A* = Accepting your thoughts and feelings and staying rooted in the here and now, observing the inner world with an attitude of flexibility, compassion, and tentativeness.
- *C* = Committing to a set of values to guide your life, rather than relying on fluctuating thoughts and feelings to determine the roads you intentionally travel down.
- *T* = Taking action, connected to your values.

As the above acronyms reveal, moving from *FEAR* to *ACT* results in action, accepting unpleasant inner events in order to live the life you want, walking down the paths that are most important to you as you place one foot in front of the other, with your shoes actually making contact with the pavement.

To act, based on your values, *willingness* is especially important. With willingness, you are fully accepting your inner world, with an attitude of non-judgment and compassion, allowing inner experiences to simply be as they are. Given that the alternative—fusion and avoidance—has likely led to a life filled with a "missing out" experience, resulting in "pain on top of pain" (Hayes, 2005), you are probably ready to pursue a different approach.

To be willing, you will continue to practice the previously explored processes, defusing from thoughts, accepting painful feelings, connecting to the observing self, and staying rooted in each moment. These ACT processes are especially important because they can prepare you to take action since you are no longer fighting against the inner world. From a pragmatic perspective, the sooner you learn to make peace with the inevitability of inner pain, the more quickly you will be able to pivot towards what is right in front of you—a trail heading to a life with purpose, meaning, and vitality.

Willingness, Grace, and the Parable of the Lost Son[1]
In Luke 15, Jesus told the story of the lost son, who impatiently asked for his share of the family fortune, quickly scurrying off on his own. Just as soon as his father could hand over the money, the son scampered away, wasting his inheritance on the pursuit of pleasure. At a certain point in the story, the son eventually realized what he had done, experienced a tremendous sense of regret, and decided to return home. In fact, when he made the choice to travel back to his father's house, he likely felt tremendous shame, given the mistakes he had made out in the world.

Still, recognizing he needed to head in a different direction, the prodigal son made the difficult trek back home. Off in the distance, he noticed his father outside, compassionately running towards him in spite of what he had done with his father's money. Even more surprising, the father ended up celebrating the son's return, grateful that his lost son was now safely back home again.

In this famous story, the lost son was determined to head back home, and his father welcomed him with open arms, paralleling humankind's relationship with God. As God patiently waits for your return, he hopes to celebrate with you, accepting you into his outstretched arms, regardless of what you have unknowingly experienced or intentionally done. In other words, one of the most important parts of this story involves God's grace and mercy, always available to anyone who is ready to return home, traveling back onto the path that heads towards God.

Interestingly, grace is commonly described as an undue merit or favor, meaning that God loves his creation in spite of humankind's wayward, wandering behaviors. Along the paths of life, you will most certainly get lost, but you can quickly return home at each and every turn. Even after spending all the proverbial money that has been given to you, God has outstretched arms and is ready to celebrate your reunion.

Having the willingness to continue turning towards home, despite the pain you may be feeling, is an especially important part of the Christian walk. Enduring the pain of the inner world, certainly, is more easily tolerable when you experience God's grace, reminiscent of the son's encounter with his father, who offered inviting, loving arms. To rest in God's embrace, then, is about letting the pain simply be, without judgment, knowing you are in his perfect care—you are home.

To view the Parable of the Lost Son through the lens of ACT, although the son had lost contact with his values, he made the courageous decision to head back home, in spite of the pain that he carried along the way. Stated differently, he made room for the shame that he felt, knowing that returning home was the right choice, consistent with the life he wanted to live. As he walked home, seeing his loving father in the distance, he may have been able to make room for whatever inner experiences arose, given that his father's grace covered them all.

In your life, if you can, try to reflect on God's grace. How, if at all, have you been able to return home after a series of mistakes, basking in God's open arms, accepting whatever inner experiences have arisen because of your firm commitment to restoring your relationship with him? In other words, are you able to make room for difficult inner pain more readily when you experience God's grace, recognizing that his outstretched arms are all that you need? Are you able to relate to your distress differently, knowing you are with your Lord, celebrating with him?

From an ACT perspective, inner experiences are embraced for pragmatic reasons—the alternative, avoidance, simply does not work if life is about living out a set of well-defined values. As a Christian, though, God's grace offers you the opportunity to fully accept whatever inner experiences arise, given that there is nothing you can do to earn his favor. Put differently, your unilateral control efforts can be relinquished, accepting God's sovereignty in place of a strategy that does not end up working in the long run. Because God freely offers you this merit, you can let go of your own tendency to compulsively manage or avoid painful thoughts, feelings, and sensations, surrendering the inner world to him from moment to moment. In turn, following Jesus becomes much more doable, with God's grace functioning as the proverbial fuel for your road trip on the streets of life.

Committed Action and Grace: A Unique Perspective from the Apostle Paul

To offer one more example of the overlap between ACT's processes and grace, especially ACT's committed action and the Bible's notion of undeserved merit, Paul mentioned in 2 Corinthians 12:7–10 that God's grace was especially important as he suffered from a "thorn" that would not go away:

- "Therefore, in order to keep me from becoming conceited, I was given a *thorn in my flesh* [italics added], a messenger of Satan, to torment me. Three times I pleaded with the Lord to take it away from me. But he said to me, 'My grace is sufficient for you, for my power is made perfect in weakness.' Therefore, I will boast all the more gladly about my weaknesses so that Christ's power may rest on me. That is why, for Christ's sake, I delight in weaknesses, in insults, in hardships, in persecutions, in difficulties. For when I am weak, then I am strong."

Consistent with the ACT model, Paul argued for the importance of grace in enduring painful experiences, given that his relationship with Jesus sustained him. For Paul, his "thorn" was a significant source of "torment." Yet, he was able to make room for it, accepting its presence and reframing it as an avenue to which he could depend on God's providential care.

In a similar vein, ACT suggests that life is about pressing forward, accepting the inner world in order to live out a set of values in the outer world. Viewed through the lens of ACT, Paul made peace with his pain, reaching for God in the process, given that he conceptualized the pain as a way to draw closer to God. With his reframe, Paul became willing to march forward, rather than stuck on the sidelines of life, preoccupied with his "thorn."

In your own life, as you struggle with the symptoms of an emotional disorder, is it possible to "delight in weaknesses," recognizing that you are strong because of God's grace? Given that God is sustaining you, can you commit to a valued direction and take action, drawing from God's strength, rather than your own efforts? To continue to explore this dynamic, it may be helpful to turn to the writings and experiences of early desert Christians, before highlighting Jesus' model of committed action in the face of pain and suffering.

Early Desert Christians and Virtue-Based Action

For early desert Christians, life was about following Jesus, enduring within the cell to deepen their relationship with God. Along the way, they strived towards living out biblical virtues, looking to God for guidance as they humbly sought to love one another. The following quote from Abba John Colobos in the *Sayings of the Desert Fathers*[2] seems to best capture virtue-based action in the desert life:

- "Personally, I would like a person to participate in all the virtues. So when you arise at dawn each day, make a fresh start in every virtue and commandment of God with greatest patience, with fear and long-suffering, in the love of God, with all spiritual and physical fervor, and with much humiliation; enduring affliction of the heart and prevention, with much prayer and intercession, with groans, in purity of the tongue and custody of the eyes; being reviled and not getting angry, living peaceably and not giving back evil for evil; not noticing the faults of others; not measuring oneself, but for you to be beneath the whole of creation, having renounced material goods and the things that pertain to the flesh; on a cross, in combat, in poverty of spirit, in determination and spiritual asceticism; in fasting, in repentance, in weeping, in the strife of battle, in discretion, in purity of the soul, in generous sharing, [doing] your manual labor in *hesychia*, in nightly vigils, in hunger and thirst, in cold and nakedness, in toils."

Although this is quite a long list of virtues, the central theme seems to be perseverance, continuing to push forward, despite a variety of hardships and painful experiences. When pressing on, loving God is a central aim, as is humility, forgiveness, non-judgment, detachment, generosity, and charity. Interestingly, notice that virtue-based living is intermingled with pain, rather than some sort of behavior that is divorced from the difficulties that life brings.

As you read through the above quote, see if you can imagine what it might be like to actually live out the virtues mentioned by Abba John, following Jesus in the midst of psychological pain. In other words, given early desert Christians' devotion to Jesus, they were especially prepared to make room for unpleasant inner experiences. In your own life, is it possible to open up inside, allowing God to offer his grace as you walk with Jesus? Rather than warring with unpleasant thoughts, feelings, and sensations, is it possible to focus on Jesus, following him where he would have you go? What follows is a brief review of Jesus' model of self-sacrifice and endurance, which may help you to draw from his strength, making room for Jesus because of your own weaknesses, reminiscent of Paul's experience of the "thorn."

Jesus and Virtue-Based Action

For Jesus, life was about virtue-based action. In fact, he frequently modeled a life of service and self-sacrifice (Tan, 2006). Throughout his short time on this planet, Jesus taught his followers to place an emphasis on loving others, dying on a cross to reconcile humankind to God. Therefore, within the Christian faith, Jesus is the embodiment of virtuous living.

In your own life, it may be especially important to get to know Jesus as you follow him, studying his life and teachings in the gospel accounts in order to better understand the life he has called you to live. Among other virtues, Jesus seemed to model humility, love, kindness, gentleness, self-control, forgiveness, and perseverance. As a result, following him as your rabbi, Messiah, and suffering servant—in fact, as the Son of God—means cultivating a meaningful life, filled with moral behaviors that emanate from the heart.

As Jesus displayed this moral behavior in the 1st century, he was especially committed to carrying out the will of God. When discussing the importance of doing the will of God, the Lutheran theologian Dietrich Bonhoeffer (1955) offered the following:

- "It is evident that the only appropriate conduct of men before God is the doing of his will. The sermon on the mount is there for the purpose of being done. Only in doing can there be submission to the will of God. In doing God's will man renounces every right and every justification of his own: he delivers himself humbly into the hands of the merciful judge. If the holy scripture insists with such urgency on doing, that is because it wishes to take away from man every possibility of self-justification before God on the basis of his own knowledge of good and evil" (p. 46).

Here, Bonhoeffer asserted that there is a significant difference between self-derived, fused knowledge—a sort of legal system of beliefs, divorced from loving action—and yielding to God's will, following Jesus along the way. In fact, for Bonhoeffer, virtue-based action is always about following a person, Jesus Christ (see, e.g., John 15:5).

In your life, how can you move from viewing Jesus' Sermon on the Mount in abstract terms, relying solely on your evaluations and "knowledge" about Jesus' teachings, to living out forgiveness, prayer, non-judgment, serving others, and so on? Which strategies in this workbook can you employ so that you can cultivate a willingness to radically follow Jesus, even though you might still experience distressing thoughts and painful feelings? Although you will come up with a more formal plan in a subsequent section of this chapter, for now, simply try to imagine how you might push forward, courageously enduring inner pain to do the will of God, following Jesus in an authentic, vibrant manner.

Martha and Virtue-Based Action

In the story of Mary and Martha in the Gospel of Luke, Mary patiently sat at the feet of Jesus, listening intently to him. On the other hand, Martha focused on serving Jesus. Her act of service was not the problem, to be sure. Instead, she seemed to be anxiously driven, what Williams (2008) referred to as the "doing" mode of the mind. In the "doing" mode, you are focused on fixing and problem solving, attempting to come up with ways to improve your inner world in the present moment. In this state, you are primarily focused on the past or the future, rather than simply "being" in the here and now, accepting the inner world with open curiosity.

Interestingly, before the story of Mary and Martha in the 10th chapter of Luke's gospel, Jesus offered a parable about a "good Samaritan." This famous traveler noticed that another was wounded, responding by bandaging the wounded man's injuries and taking him to an inn to be nursed back to health. These two stories in Luke—the Parable of the Good Samaritan and Mary and Martha's time spent with Jesus—seem to capture the blend of contemplation and action in the Christian life (Cutler, 2003). After all, Jesus stated that loving God and others are essential qualities for those who want to experience eternal life (see Luke 10:25–28).

In your life, how can you move from fusion and avoidance to applying contemplation and the Mary mode to the inner world and Martha and virtue-based action in the outer world? Combining the two, what might your life look like if you were both responsive to those in need—like the Samaritan—and able to sit at the feet of Jesus to find rest and deepen your relationship with him? Overall, this amalgamation can be especially relevant to your current struggle with an emotional disorder, given ACT's emphasis on value-based living, rather than the total elimination of psychological pain.

What follows are some virtue-based action metaphors, emphasizing a willingness to press forward, despite the pain you are in. Within faith-based ACT, the purpose for life is cultivating a deeper awareness of God's active, loving presence so that you can be more accepting of inner pain, pivoting towards following Jesus, rather than waiting on the "sidelines of life" for inner distress to go away. Reminiscent of Jesus' disciples, who responded to his call, Jesus is asking for you to walk with him, living out his teachings as you learn to love more fully, receiving his grace and mercy along the way.

Virtue-Based Action Metaphors

- Jesus continued to pursue his father's will, even when he faced an excruciatingly painful execution, yielding to God's plan for his life. In my life, I can trust God, pressing forward by emulating Jesus, even though my inner distress is still present.
- After Jesus' death, resurrection, and ascension, both Paul and Peter shared the gospel message, even though they experienced tremendous suffering and hardship in the New Testament. In my day to day experiences, I can continue, recognizing that Jesus is with me as I endure my inner pain to follow him.

- Even though Peter denied Jesus in the gospels, he quickly got back on track, following Jesus in spite of the mistake he made. When it comes to my life, I can acknowledge my inner distress, pivoting towards Jesus when I realize that I have drifted away due to fusion or avoidance.[3]

- Although Moses faced extremely difficult environmental conditions, he pushed on, leading God's people through the desert for several decades, trusting in God's plan. In my life, I might sometimes feel lost and confused, especially when I am struggling with inner pain; yet, I can continue to trust in God, following him when I feel like I am wandering in the desert. Rather than turning around, wanting to head back to captivity and enslavement, I can continue to head in God's direction—the Promised Land.

- For Noah, he was willing to spend years building an ark, even though he did not fully understand God's plan for him. Still, Noah yielded to God's will, with God blessing him and his family by saving them from the flood. In my life, I can continue to follow Jesus, even when I do not know what awaits me, trusting in God's providence as I emulate Jesus' behavior from moment to moment.

- Like the Parable of the Lost Son, I can head home each and every time I notice I have drifted, running down the roads of life to a God, who has outstretched arms, ready to celebrate with me upon my return. When I experience tremendous psychological pain, I can still follow God's plan, trusting that he is with me, even though I may feel shame, like the Lost Son.

In each of these examples, the central theme is virtue-based action. Even though a wide variety of biblical characters felt afraid, angry, sad, or ashamed, they courageously stayed the course, turning towards God, rather than away from him.

Virtue-Based Action and Emotional Disorders

Within the ACT model, avoiding life causes much more suffering than the symptoms you are currently experiencing (Hayes, 2005). Therefore, the emphasis is on making room for unpleasant inner experiences, rather than fighting against them, given that the battle with inner pain only distracts you from building the life you want. As you practice defusion, acceptance, connecting to the observing self, and staying rooted in the here and now, you may find that you are no longer preoccupied with pain eradication, and can focus, instead, on the roads ahead.

As you shift your focus from being preoccupied with what is going on inside of your vehicle to the road that is outside of your car, you will find that you now need a map to put the car in drive and head in an intentional direction. This map, captured via value-based living, can help you to decide which roads to choose as your foot is pressing down on the gas pedal. Certainly, having a map can help you develop and live out a set of goals that are consistent with what matters most to you in this life.

Yet, if you do not have the determination to press your foot on the gas pedal, your car will remain in one place, even though you might have a very detailed map, capturing a "helicopter view" of your geographic location. Deciding to hit the gas pedal, rather than staying in park, is the most important part of the journey, especially if you have already learned to accept (with an open curiosity) what goes on inside the car, letting go of some of the distractions that have sidetracked you thus far.

The "action" part of "virtue-based action" means that you are deciding to press forward courageously, consistent with Jesus' model of service and self-sacrifice, even though you know there will be pain ahead. Given that Jesus was connected to the will of God, he was focused on the path God had carved out for him. His willingness to push on, even though there was tremendous suffering around the corner, was rooted in an intimate, loving union with his father.

In your life, as you cultivate a more loving, trusting relationship with God, you may find that you can make room for inner pain more easily, recognizing that God is sovereign, guiding your paths. In your time alone with God, you might begin to recognize that you do not have to eradicate your pain fully to walk with Jesus, based on the notion that God will provide as you trek across the land to live out a set of moral behaviors that emulate Jesus. This journey, of course, is special because of the traveling companion you are walking next to, even if your feet hurt and your muscles are fatigued.

Whether you are dealing with a low mood, thoughts of "worthlessness," anxiety about an uncertain future, or panic-related symptoms, God is with you; therefore, you can yield to his will, trusting that he has a plan for both your inner and outer world. One way to conceptualize the inner-outer distinction, including how acceptance and action can work together, comes from Jesus' teaching in the Gospel of Luke. What follows is an exercise to help you continue to develop virtue-based action even when your pain is still present, lingering around from moment to moment.

Exercise: The Vine and the Branches
In John 15:1–8, Jesus taught about the "Vine and the Branches," noted below:

- "I am the true vine, and my Father is the gardener. He cuts off every branch in me that bears no fruit, while every branch that does bear fruit he prunes so that it will be even more fruitful. You are already clean because of the word I have spoken to you. Remain in me, as I also remain in you. No branch can bear fruit by itself; it must remain in the vine. Neither can you bear fruit unless you remain in me. I am the vine; you are the branches. If you remain in me and I in you, you will bear much fruit; apart from me, you can do nothing. If you do not remain in me, you are like a branch that is thrown away and withers; such branches are picked up, thrown into the fire and burned. If you remain in me, and my words remain in you, ask whatever you wish, and it will be done for you. This is to my Father's glory, that you bear much fruit, showing yourselves to be my disciples."

In this section of the Bible, Jesus outlined the relationship that Christians are to have with him. In your life, Jesus is the source, with moral behavior organically flowing from your relationship with him. Therefore, it is especially important to emphasize that virtue-based action involves connecting to the supplier—Jesus Christ—from moment to moment, rather than heading in your direction to pursue self-derived values.

This central teaching, rooted in the Christian tradition, is what distinguishes traditional ACT from a faith-based version of ACT. Because of this, when you recognize that you are following your set of values, rather than remaining in Jesus (the vine) as the branch, you have the opportunity to return home, reminiscent of the Lost Son. It may be important to spend a bit more time on this, envisioning that you are truly connected to Jesus as the source.

When you are ready, close your eyes and imagine that Jesus is the vine. You are connected to him, extending out of the vine as one of his branches. In fact, you can give glory to God by simply functioning as a branch (Merton, 1961), connected to your source and growing in the bright blue sky. Now, try to imagine stretching out your leaves towards the sun, attached to Jesus as the vine. With each passing day, try to envision that Jesus is with you, offering you nourishment, consistent with a vine passing on nutrients to its branches. Just sit for a few minutes in silence, imagining that Jesus is giving you the fuel to grow because he is your source.

When you are finished, see if you can write down some of your thoughts. What was it like to imagine Jesus as your literal source, supplying you with the requisite strength to live out your God-given purpose? In daily living, how can you apply Jesus' teachings, recognizing that he guides your paths and offers you the strength to press forward? Given that he is the source, can you make room for difficult inner experiences with more hope and endurance?

_____

_____

_____

_____

_____

_____

_____

_____

_____

_____

Exercise: Writing Your Own Gospel Account

Rather than presenting a purely abstract understanding of virtue-based living, ACT consistently emphasizes the importance of viewing values as actual behaviors. In fact, values can be especially salient when they are rooted in an "all or nothing" attitude (Hayes et al., 2012), living out a set of principles, instead of just knowing *about* them. For this reason, building on the last chapter, you may find it useful to think about following Jesus—guided by virtue-based action—behaviorally, rather than abstractly, in some distant, far away land.

Interestingly, in the New Testament, the gospel of Mark seems to especially emphasize Jesus' ministry and deeds (Achtemeier, Green, & Thompson, 2001). For example, Mark documented Jesus' various healings, as well as feeding large groups of people. Although the author of Mark did offer an actual narrative, explicating Jesus' identity as the Messiah, much of the account illuminated Jesus' observable behaviors (Achtemeier et al., 2001). As a result, consistent with the gospel of Mark, see if you can write a behaviorally-oriented account of what your life will look like following Jesus over the course of the next month. Again, rather than thinking about virtues in an abstract way, try to be as concrete as possible, documenting what you will do as you follow Jesus, reminiscent of Mark's style of writing about Jesus' life and interactions with others.

_____

_____

_____

_____

_____

_____

_____

_____

_____

_____

_____

_____

_____

Exercise: Are You Willing to Walk on Water?[4]

In Matthew 14:25–33, Jesus' disciples saw him walking on water in the distance, with Peter confidently asking to come see Jesus out on the lake:

- "Shortly before dawn Jesus went out to them, walking on the lake. When the disciples saw him walking on the lake, they were terrified. 'It's a ghost,' they said, and cried out in fear. But Jesus immediately said to them: 'Take courage! It is I. Don't be afraid.' 'Lord, if it's you,' Peter replied, 'tell me to come to you on the water.' 'Come,' he said. Then Peter got down out of the boat, walked on the water and came toward Jesus. But when he saw the wind, he was afraid and, beginning to sink, cried out, 'Lord, save me!' Immediately Jesus reached out his hand and caught him. 'You of little faith,' he said, 'why did you doubt?' And when they climbed into the boat, the wind died down. Then those who were in the boat worshiped him, saying, 'Truly you are the Son of God.'"

In this account, Peter seemed to be originally filled with courage, willing to walk directly to Jesus to follow him. As he took his eyes off Jesus, his mind started to generate doubts, noticing some of the barriers to reaching his destination. As he observed the wind blowing, he started to sink, with Jesus rescuing him with an extended hand.

Interestingly, you may find there are immediate parallels with your life here. Virtue-based action is similar to Peter boldly following Jesus, asking to come and see him on the water. As Peter was focused on Jesus' presence, he was able to head to his desired destination. Still, because he started to get caught up in his mind, likely with seeds of doubt, he lost his focus, sinking in the process.

As you apply this story to your life, try to envision what it would be like to courageously get out on the water to meet Jesus, trusting in Jesus as you walked towards him. In the process, there will most certainly be difficult inner experiences that will arise, consistent with Peter's doubt. However, staying focused on him can help you continue to march forward, receiving Jesus' outstretched hand. Even if you begin to sink, similar to wandering off the path of virtue-based action, Jesus is with you, offering his support as he pulls you safely to the boat.

Now, if you can, try to imagine focusing exclusively on Jesus as you walk towards him, allowing your thoughts and feelings to run their natural course, without buying into possible seeds of doubt or distressing feelings. Rather, see if you can continue to walk forward, bringing your inner experiences along for the ride. In the space that follows, see if you can list out some of the barriers, reminiscent of Peter's doubt, which might lead to a sinking experience. Then, see if you can list several ways to refocus on Jesus, drawing from some of the exercises throughout this workbook that you have learned and practiced.

Thoughts and Feelings That Might Arise as I Walk to Jesus on the Water	
Strategies, Exercises, and Metaphors I Can Use to Stay Focused on Jesus When I Notice I am Beginning to Sink	

Exercise: Barriers to Action

Within ACT, life is about taking action, rooted in a set of well defined values to guide each step of the way. On the roads of life, there will be some obstacles, including potholes, manholes, and the like. In other words, you will experience a wide variety of inner and outer barriers to value-based living. Given that these types of distractions are inevitable, you may find it helpful to begin to identify some of your thoughts, feelings, and sensations that might momentarily distract you from virtue-based living. Therefore, please fill in the sections in the below box (adapted from Harris, 2009), integrating your work from both the last chapter and this chapter:

Virtues I Will Live By as I Follow Jesus	
Virtues (rooted in the Bible)	
Goals (measurable, attainable, positive, and specific)	
Behaviors (concrete, observable steps I will take)	
Inner Distress I Will Endure With Hope and Patience In Order to Follow Jesus	
Thoughts	
Feelings	

Sensations	
Memories/Images	
Faith-Based ACT Strategies/Exercises/Metaphors I Will Utilize to Follow Jesus	
Defusion/Watchfulness	
Acceptance/Endurance	
Present-Moment Awareness/Silence and Stillness With God	
The Observing Self/The Contemplative Self	

Exercise: *FEAR* and *ACT* for Christians

To offer a modified version of the *FEAR* (the problem) and *ACT* (the solution) acronyms (adapted from Hayes et al., 2012), see the following, which can be applied to daily Christian living:

- *F* = Fusing with the *logismoi*, leaning on your understanding, rather than trusting in God's plan for your life.
- *E* = Evaluating your inner experiences as "bad," struggling to trust in God's providential care.
- *A* = Avoiding following Jesus, telling him you will catch up with him just as soon as the symptoms go away.
- *R* = Reason giving, offering "valid" excuses why you will not be able to follow Jesus until some later point in time because of your current psychological pain.

- *A* = Accepting your thoughts and feelings because God is sovereign, surrendering inner distress to him and focusing on his active, loving present from moment to moment.
- *C* = Committing to biblical virtues as a "map" for life, emulating Jesus, rather than relying on fluctuating thoughts and feelings to determine the direction you take in life.
- *T* = Taking action, connected to biblical virtues and serving others, like Jesus.

Exercise: Jesus Has Prepared a Place for You

In the Gospel of John (14:1–4), Jesus mentioned to his disciples that he was going to prepare a place for them in heaven:

- "Do not let your hearts be troubled. You believe in God; believe also in me. My Father's house has many rooms; if that were not so, would I have told you that I am going there to prepare a place for you? And if I go and prepare a place for you, I will come back and take you to be with me that you also may be where I am. You know the way to the place where I am going."

As this workbook comes to a close, in this exercise, I would like for you to imagine that you have lived a long, fruitful life, following Jesus each step of the way. There were moments, certainly, that have involved sinking and wandering, reminiscent of Peter's struggle to fully follow Jesus in each and every moment. Overall, you were able to follow Jesus faithfully, walking with him as he helped you navigate the difficult terrain of the world.

In heaven, Jesus has prepared a place for you, and has called you home. As you settle in to your new home, you are able to reflect with him on your experience, reminiscing about your time spent walking with him. In the space that follows, see if you can describe the life you would have liked to live, including the virtues—emanating from your heart—which you would have liked to display in your relationship with God and others. How did you display, in behavioral terms, the virtues that Jesus taught you about? How did you emulate Jesus in daily living? Among some of the virtues explored in the last few chapters, how did you make them your own, demonstrating your love for God and others by exhibiting these moral behaviors? How were you able to endure difficult inner experiences in order to confidently walk with Jesus? What role did God play in the process, strengthening and sustaining you as you pressed forward?

_____

_____

_____

_____

_____

_____

_____

_____

_____

_____

_____

_____

_____

_____

_____

Now, what will it take to begin to live out these virtues—right here and right now? In fact, Jesus is knocking on your door in this very moment, if you will slow down to listen. Are you willing to set down your pen right now to answer the knock on the door? Right now is the time, given that there is no other time than now. Can you get up, walk to the door, and invite him in so as to begin your new journey?

- "Here I am! I stand at the door and knock. If anyone hears my voice and opens the door, I will come in and eat with that person, and they with me" (Revelation 3:20).

Conclusion

In this workbook, you have explored a wide variety of ACT strategies, metaphors, and exercises, rooted in six processes. These processes are designed to help you live out your values, creating a life that truly matters to you, rather than waiting for your pain to go away. Given that life is most certainly painful and difficult, you have worked on ways to make room for unpleasant inner experiences in order to shift your focus towards behaviors that can enhance this life that God has offered you.

As a Christian, you also explored ways to integrate ACT's processes with the Christian tradition, drawing from the Bible and the experiences and sayings of early desert Christians. In fact, with faith-based ACT (Knabb, 2016), the central goal is to cultivate a deeper awareness of God's active, loving presence to follow Jesus, your rabbi and suffering servant. Along the paths of life, you will inevitably experience pain; yet, as you walk with Jesus, you can trust that he will be with you, guiding you towards pursuing God's will.

By practicing watchfulness, endurance, stillness and silence with God, and the ability to connect to God directly, you are on your way to creating the life that God wants for you, following God's one and only Son along the rugged trails of this life. In that faith-based ACT is ultimately about a relationship, rather than a list of virtues, plugging into the source from moment to moment can allow you to find rest, strength, and comfort during your most difficult times.

As someone who currently struggles with an emotional disorder, you may be especially exhausted from trying to fight against inner distress. Still, because Jesus' "yoke is easy" and "burden is light" (Matthew 11:30), he offers you "living water" to quench your thirst (John 4:14). Whether you feel like you are being tempted in the wilderness (Matthew 4:1–11), or fatigued because you are carrying your cross (Matthew 16:24), Jesus empathizes with your weaknesses and is waiting on the throne (Hebrews 4:14–16), offering you grace and mercy with his outstretched arms (Luke 15:11–32).

May God bless you on your continued journey, living a long life in full devotion to him, finishing the race strong, with zeal, passion, and excitement (2 Timothy 4:7):

- "I have fought the good fight, I have finished the race, I have kept the faith."

Notes

1 Worth mentioning, Hayes et al. (2012) briefly discussed the overlap between acceptance and grace, although they did not fully develop this intersection.

2 The saying in this section is quoted from Wortley (2012). Used with permission.

3 This metaphor is influenced by Wilson and DuFrene's (2010) example of Peter's struggle to live out his faith in the gospel accounts.

4 This exercise is influenced by Wilson and DuFrene's (2010) example of Peter's struggle to live out his faith in the gospel accounts.

References

Achtemeier, P., Green, J., & Thompson, M. (2001). *Introducing the New Testament: Its Literature and Theology.* Grand Rapids, MI: Wm. B. Eerdmans Publishing Company.

Bonhoeffer, D. (1955). *Ethics.* New York: Touchstone.

Cutler, D. (2003). *Western Mysticism: Augustine, Gregory and Bernard on Contemplation and the Contemplative Life.* New York: Dover Publications, Inc.

Harris, R. (2009). *ACT Made Simple. An Easy-to-Read Primer on Acceptance and Commitment Therapy.* Oakland, CA: New Harbinger Publications, Inc.

Hayes, S. (2005). *Get Out of Your Mind and Into Your Life: The New Acceptance & Commitment Therapy.* Oakland, CA: New Harbinger Publications, Inc.

Hayes, S., Strosahl, K., & Wilson, K. (2012). *Acceptance and Commitment Therapy: The Process and Practice of Mindful Change* (2nd ed.). New York: The Guilford Press.

Knabb, J. (2016). *Faith-Based ACT for Christian Clients: An Integrative Treatment Approach.* New York: Routledge.

Merton, T. (1961). *New Seeds of Contemplation.* New York: New Directions Books.

Tan, S. (2006). *Full Service: Moving from Self-Service Christianity to Total Servanthood.* Grand Rapids, MI: Baker Books.

Williams, M. (2008). *Mindfulness, depression and modes of mind. Cognitive Therapy Research, 32,* 721–733.

Wilson, K., & DuFrene, T. (2010). *Things Might Go Terribly, Horribly Wrong: A Guide to Life Liberated from Anxiety.* Oakland, CA: New Harbinger Publications, Inc.

Wortley, J. (2012). *The Book of Elders: Sayings of the Desert Fathers.* Trappist, KY: Cistercian Publications.

Index

acceptance 4, 29, 37–38, 43; action and
10–12, 69–72; defined 8
acceptance and commitment therapy
(ACT): acceptance process 8,
69–72; ACT acronym 154–5,
169–70; anxiety disorders and
20; Christian counseling and 2;
cognitive defusion 45–50, 51,
54, 56, 65; committed action 8,
154–5; defusion 4, 7; exercises in
13, 22–27, 32–33, 39–41, 49–50,
57–65, 76–86, 96–106, 119–27, 135–7,
141–50, 164–71; externalizing the
mind 48–49, 58–59; FEAR acronym
154–5, 169; goals 13; language
and 46–47; metaphors 48–49,
56–57, 75–76, 97–98, 141–2, 161–2;
mindfulness in 90–92; observing
self and 8, 109–14; present-moment
awareness 8, 89–93, 96; processes
of 4–5; stillness and silence 97–98;
values and 8, 20, 130–2; virtues
and 147–8
ACT. *See* acceptance and commitment
therapy (ACT)
ACT acronym 154–5, 169–70
active life 11
Adam 6, 21, 57, 102
Alcohol Anonymous 38
anger 70
anxiety 70

anxiety disorders: mindfulness and 91;
prevalence of 17–18; sense of self
117; symptoms of 17–20, 23–24;
virtues and 140
apophatic prayer 81, 110
attention 90
avoidance 10
avoidance strategies 1–2, 4, 6,
29–43. *See also* experiential
avoidance (EA)

behavioral avoidance 31
being mode 11–12, 54, 85–86, 118–19,
139, 160
being still 79–80
Bible 2; experiential avoidance in 33–34;
hopeful endurance *(hupomone)*
73–74; metaphors 35–36; suffering
and 6, 21–23; theological virtues
138, 144–5; watchfulness in 52–54
Biblical values 127
Biblical virtues 127
Bonhoeffer, Dietrich 159–60
breathing, mindful 102–3

cataphatic prayer 81
cease striving *(raphah)* 79
cell. *See also* desert Christians: God in
50–51, 72–73, 78; as inner world
93–94; monastic life in 34–35, 50–51;
symbolic 78–79

Centering Prayer 80–84, 102–3
Christian clients 12–13
Christian counselling: acceptance and
commitment therapy 2; experiential
avoidance (EA) and 31–32;
Jesus Christ in 2
Christianity: acceptance and
commitment therapy (ACT) 9–10;
contemplative 115
Christian life: contemplation and
161; following Jesus 6–7, 12, 21,
25–27, 139–41; hopeful endurance
(hupomone) 73–74; value based
169–70; virtues and 132–5;
watchfulness *(nepsis)* 52–54
Christian mindfulness 12, 92–93
"clean" pain 35–36
cognitive defusion in ACT process
45–50, 51, 54, 56, 65
Colobos, Abba John 158
committed action 8; defined 5, 153;
exercises 164–71; grace and 157–8;
metaphors 161–2
compass metaphor 131
contemplative Christianity:
acceptance-based therapy 8, 10; Mary
and 10–11, 117; stillness *(hesychia)*
93–96; watchfulness *(nepsis)* 50–52
contemplative prayer 9–10, 80–84;
focus on Christ and 114–15;
present-moment awareness 85–86

Index

contemplative self 109, 114–15;
    metaphors 120–1
creative hopelessness 37–38, 40, 43

defusion 4, 7
denial as experiential avoidance (EA) 32
depressive disorders: mindfulness and
    91; relapse of 18; sense of self 117;
    symptoms of 18; virtues and 140
desert Christians 7, 10, 21, 45;
    avoidance and acceptance 34–35;
    contemplative self and 114–15;
    eye of the soul (nous) 114; hopeful
    endurance (hupomone) 73; stillness
    and silence with God 93–96;
    temptations and 55, 73;
    virtue-based action 158–9;
    virtues and 132–3, 135–6, 153;
    watchfulness (nepsis)
    50–52, 65
desert psychology 2, 8, 10, 21
detachment 135–7
devil 52, 53, 56, 125
dialetical behavior therapy (DBT) 3
dianoia 114, 117, 127
"dirty" pain 35–36
discerning 57
distraction as experiential avoidance
    (EA) 31
distress 20. See also emotional disorders
distress aversion 31
doing mode 11, 118–19, 139, 160

Egypt 57
emotional acceptance 70–72
emotional avoidance 70–71, 76–77
emotional disorders 1, 6, 10;
    characteristics 17–20; contemplative
    self and 117–18; mindfulness and 91;
    stillness and silence 97; virtue-based
    action and 162–3; virtues and 140–1;
    watchfulness and 55
endurance. See hopeful endurance
    (hupomone)

Evagrius, Ponticus 50, 53, 114, 133
Eve 6, 21, 57
evil thoughts (logismoi) 55, 65–66, 94,
    115, 127, 133
exercises 10, 32–33, 49–50, 57–65,
    76–86, 98–106, 119–27, 135–7,
    141–50, 164–71
experiential avoidance (EA): ACT
    exercises 32–33; Biblical 33–34;
    definition 29–30; identifying 32–33;
    social isolation and 37;
    types of 31–32
exposure therapy 84–85
externalizing the mind 48–49, 58–59
eye of the soul (nous) 8, 109, 114–19, 127

faith 2, 138
false self 124–6
FEAR acronym 154–5, 169
fusion 46

Garden of Eden 6, 33, 56, 57
Garden of Gethsemane 76
generalized anxiety disorder (GAD):
    experiential avoidance (EA)
    and 31; symptoms of 19–20;
    worry and 30
Genesis 33
goals linked to virtues 149–50
God: in the cell 50–51, 72–73, 78;
    contemplative prayer and 9, 81–82,
    110; dependence on 40–41, 56;
    experiencing 119–20; eye of the soul
    (nous) and 114–15, 117–18; grace of
    156–8; lament to 41–42; presence
    of 9; present-moment awareness
    94–95; as sovereign 163; standing
    before 146; suffering and 6–7;
    surrendering to 9, 33–34, 38, 40–41,
    62–64, 83; trust in 21–22, 59–60;
    will of 159
Good Samaritan parable 161
grace 156–8
guilt 70

happiness, pursuit of 11
hesychia. See stillness (hesychia)
hope 138
hopeful endurance (hupomone) 8, 66,
    73–74; Mary mode and 74–75;
    metaphors 75–78
human suffering. See suffering
hupomone. See hopeful endurance
    (hupomone)

impairment of functioning 20
inner stillness 93–96
Israel 41
Israelites 57

Jeremiah 22
Jesus Christ 1; asking for mercy from
    97; in Christian counselling 2;
    experiencing 122–4; experiencing
    pain 35–36; following 8, 12, 18, 21,
    25–27, 64, 137–8, 142–3, 147–8, 153–4,
    167; Martha and 54, 74, 85; Mary and
    38, 54, 61, 74–75, 85, 160; preparing
    a place 170–1; Sermon on the
    Mount 135, 139–40, 145–6; suffering
    and 5–7, 69, 76; surrendering
    to 60; teachings of 140–1, 145–6;
    temptation and 56, 125; virtue-based
    action and 159–60; walking on water
    166–7; watchful and 53
Jesus Prayer 45, 50–51, 60–61, 65, 95–96,
    101–2, 115, 117, 126–7, 134
John (clinical example) 3
Jonah 33
Judas 56
judgmental statements 46, 57–58

knowledge of good and evil 57–58

lament psalms 41–42
language: defusion exercises 49–50;
    inner dialogue 46–47; value-based
    action and 48
Lectio Divina 103–4

logismoi. See evil thoughts *(logismoi)*
Lost Son parable 76, 142, 155–7, 162
love 138
Luke 54

major depressive disorder (MDD) 30;
    experiential avoidance (EA) and 31;
    symptoms of 18
Mark, the Apostle 165–6
Martha: active life and 11, 139; Jesus
    Christ and 54, 74, 85; virtue-based
    action and 160–1
Mary 38; contemplative life and 10–11,
    117, 139; Jesus Christ and 31, 54, 61,
    74–75, 85, 160; stillness and silence
    96; watchfulness and 54
meditative exercises 49, 57–65
metanoia 110
metaphors 35–36, 48–49, 56–57, 75–78,
    97–98, 120–1, 141–2, 161–2
mindfulness 5, 10; acceptance-based
    therapy 118; anxiety disorders and
    91; characteristics of 91; Christian
    54; defined 90; depressive disorders
    and 91; emotional disorders and 91
mindfulness-based cognitive therapy
    (MBCT) 3, 118
monks 2, 7, 8–9, 73, 93–94, 97, 135–6, 140.
    See also desert Christians
morals 132
Moses 21–22, 33, 57, 162

negative self statements 46
nepsis. See watchfulness *(nepsis)*
Niebuhr, Reinhold 139
Noah 76, 100, 162
nous. See eye of the soul *(nous)*

observing self 8, 109–14; defined 5,
    109; exercises 119–27; eye of the
    soul *(nous)* and 109–10, 114–116;
    metaphors 120–1; sense of self
    and 111–13
overeating 133

pain. *See also* psychological pain:
    avoidance strategies of 1–2;
    "clean" 35–36; "dirty" 35–36
painful inner experiences 134;
    acceptance of 71–72, 155–7;
    avoiding 29–30; endurance of 4,
    8; prayer and 84–85; virtue-based
    action 162–3
panic attacks 133
panic disorder 30; experiential avoidance
    (EA) and 31; symptoms of 3–4, 19
Parable of the Good Samaritan 161
Parable of the Lost Son 76, 142,
    155–7, 162
passionlessness 133
Paul, the Apostle 22, 73–74, 76,
    157–8, 161
Peter, the Apostle 33–34, 36, 53, 56,
    142, 161–2, 167
Pharisees 56, 58, 138
Philokalia 109, 114, 115, 116
pornography 133
prayer: *apophatic* 81, 110; *cataphatic*
    81; Centering Prayer 80–84, 102–3;
    contemplative 80–84; Jesus 115;
    Jesus Prayer 45, 50–51, 60–61, 65,
    95–96, 101–2, 117, 126–7, 134; *Lectio*
    Divina 103–4; pure 114; Serenity
    Prayer 139; Welcoming Prayer 84–85
present-moment awareness 8; in ACT
    therapy 89–93; contemplative
    prayer and 85–86; defined 4
procrastination 31
Protestantism 2
psalms 41–42
psychological pain 10. *See also* painful
    inner experiences; accepting 6–7,
    75; Biblical 6, 21–23, 33–34; in
    contemporary Western society
    17–27; experiential avoidance and
    37, 39; pain of absence/presence 1–2
psychotherapy's avoidance strategies
    31–32
pure prayer 114

raphah 79
reason-based mind 114
reliving the past 46
repression as experiential avoidance
    (EA) 32
rigid rules 47, 58

sadness 70
Sayings of the Desert Fathers 7, 10, 34,
    51, 73, 93, 94, 135, 158
self-sacrifical behaviors 139
sense of self 110–14
Serenity Prayer 139
Sermon on the Mount 135, 139–40,
    145–6
servanthood 139
silence 93–96
social anxiety disorders 134;
    experiential avoidance and 30;
    symptoms of 19
social isolation 35
social phobia and experiential avoidance
    (EA) 31
staying put 35
stillness *(hesychia)* 8, 93–106; exercises
    96–106; metaphors 97–98
storied self 121–2
submission 38
suffering 1–2; Bible and 6–7; in Christian
    culture 11
suppression as experiential avoidance
    (EA) 31

Tabernacle altar 40–41
theological virtues 138
Thomas, the Apostle 56
thoughts and cognitive defusion 45–47
Tina (clinical example) 23–24

value-based action 12, 47
values: as behaviors 165–6; Christian
    146–7; daily life and 47–48, 137;
    defined 2, 5, 130; importance
    of 130–1

verbal self: over reliance on 110–11; sense of self and 109

virtue-based action 138, 143, 158–61; barriers to 168–9; emotional disorders and 162–3; metaphors 161–2

virtues 8; Biblical 129; Christian 144, 153–4; contemplative Christianity and 132–5, 139; freedom to choose 137–8; linking to goals 149–50; metaphors 141–2; as moral excellence 132; seven 133; theological 138

watchfulness (nepsis) 7, 45, 50–52, 66, 116; emotional disorders and 55; metaphors 56–57

Welcoming Prayer 84–85

willingfulness 155

worry 21–22, 30, 133